1 0 S T E P S T O

Successful
Training

Elaine Biech

ASTD PRESS
Alexandria, Virginia

ASTD Press is an internationally renowned source of insightful and practical information on workplace learning and performance topics, including training basics, evaluation and return-on-investment, instructional systems development, e-learning, leadership, and career development.

Ordering information: Books published by ASTD Press can be purchased by visiting our website at store.astd.org or by calling 800.628.2783 or 703.683.8100.

Library of Congress Control Number: 2008923895
ISBN-10: 1-56286-541-2
ISBN-13: 978-1-56286-541-2

ASTD Press Editorial Staff:
Director: Cat Russo
Manager, Acquisitions and Author Relations: Mark Morrow
Editorial Manager: Jacqueline Edlund-Braun
Senior Associate Editor: Tora Estep
Associate Editor: Maureen Soyars
Copyeditor: Pamela Lankas
Indexer: Mary Kidd
Proofreader: IGS
Interior Design and Production: International Graphics Services
Cover Design: Elizabeth Park

Printed by Victor Graphics, Inc., Baltimore, Maryland, www.victorgraphics.com

For Shane and Thad . . .

Two of My Steps to Success

Let's face it, most people spend their days in chaotic, fast-paced, time- and resource-strained organizations. Finding time for just one more project, assignment, or even learning opportunity—no matter how career enhancing or useful—is difficult to imagine. The *10-Steps* series is designed for today's busy professional who needs advice and guidance on a wide array of topics ranging from project management to people management, from business strategy to decision making and time management, from stepping in to deliver a presentation for someone else to researching and creating a compelling presentation as well as effectively delivering the content. Each book in this ASTD series promises to take its readers on a journey to basic understanding, with practical application the ultimate destination. This is truly a just-tell-me-what-to-do-now series. You will find action-driven language teamed with examples, worksheets, case studies, and tools to help you quickly implement the right steps and chart a path to your own success. The *10-Steps* series will appeal to a broad business audience from middle managers to upper-level management. Workplace learning and human resource professionals along with other professionals seeking to improve their value proposition in their organizations will find these books a great resource.

C O N T E N T S

P R E F A C E

10 Steps to Successful Training is a bit unorthodox:

- ◆ It does not follow a representative instructional systems design (ISD) process.
- ◆ It does not fill in every detail that is critical to ensure training succeeds.
- ◆ It does not try to outline all the dos and don'ts of good training.
- ◆ It doesn't even touch on all the typical topics such as the pros and cons of various visual aids, how to deal with difficult participants, or how to write objectives.

Good grief!

10 Steps to Successful Training also doesn't follow a classic training table of contents. For example, Step 3 addresses both design and delivery at the same time. And one entire step is dedicated to you, the trainer. So you see this isn't your typical, here's-the-training-cycle book.

What I have done instead is to pull out the 10 key actions trainers need to take to be successful. Yes, many other aspects are required to provide complete training design and implementation. You can find those in many of the books I have listed in the Resources at the end of this book.

10 Steps to Successful Training describes a short list of what I believe to be the critical elements needed to achieve results when you are on the line to produce. There are many aspects of training—from the assessment to the implementation and evaluation of training. So to select only 10 meant examining all of the elements and prioritizing the ones I believe have the most influence on the final success of training. The result of this effort comprises the 10 steps that you find in this book:

1. **Understand the Role of the Trainer**
2. **Align Training to Improve Your Organization's Bottom Line**
3. **Use Adult Learning Principles to Design and Deliver Training**
4. **Prepare to Succeed and Be Credible**
5. **Create a Safe and Engaging Learning Environment**
6. **Facilitate Effectively—Learning Is About Active Engagement**
7. **Present Like a Pro—Presentation Is Key**
8. **Make It Interesting—Use Lively Openings, Transitions, and Powerful Closings**
9. **Don't Forget Classic Techniques That Enhance Learning**
10. **Get Involved—Helping Others Learn Is Fun and Rewarding**

You will find a brief summary of each of the steps in the introduction. I think you will agree that these 10 steps are extremely influential in training's final results. Interestingly, in many cases these same 10 also need further development. And even though *10 Steps to Successful Training* is not written in a traditional training sequence, you will see that it addresses areas many of us in the profession need to focus on because of their importance. You will not find all the answers in this book. I do hope, however, that the *10 Steps to Successful Training* will inspire you to step back and examine what you do in each of these areas and to identify how you can improve personally and professionally, putting your focus where it counts.

Acknowledgments

10 Steps to Successful Training was authored by many wise and wonderful people. It is a delight to thank everyone who "wrote" this book:

- Consultants, trainers, and mentors who led the way and taught me all that I know: Jean Barbazette, Geoff Bellman, Ken and Margie Blanchard, Peter Block, Richard Chang, Ann Herrmann-Nehdi, Don Kirkpatrick, Jim Kouzes, Bob Pike, Dana and Jim Robinson, Ed Scannell, Mel Silberman, Thiagi, Cal Wick, and Jack Zenger.
- Mark Morrow, editor and friend, for pushing me to complete this book.
- Cat Russo, publisher, for continuing to provide me with challenging and exciting opportunities.
- Jacki Edlund-Braun, Tora Estep, Maureen Soyars, and Pamela Lankas for making this a better book.
- Lorraine Kohart, my assistant, who read and reread and took care of the details.
- Dan Greene, for putting life on hold while I wrote.
- Clients, for allowing me to practice successful training with you.

elaine biech
ebb associates, inc.
Norfolk, VA

INTRODUCTION

How do you stack up as a trainer? Do you have all the skills you believe it takes for success? While working on an earlier project, I
identified the characteristics of a successful trainer. I've listed
some of them here for you. A successful trainer is assertive and influencing, logical and creative, a trust builder, confident and
poised, customer focused, a good presenter, articulate, enthusiastic, an excellent communicator (verbal and written), flexible and
spontaneous, a good listener, impartial and objective, a lifelong
learner, patient, people-oriented, warm and approachable, process
oriented, self-sufficient, solution and results oriented, a team
player, tolerant of ambiguity, well-organized, and possessing of a
strong business sense and a good sense of humor.

As you read *10 Steps to Successful Training* you will find these
same characteristics comprise the essence of the book. For example, Step 5, Create a Safe and Engaging Learning Environment, requires more than half of the characteristics just mentioned. And
Step 10 is devoted entirely to dedicating yourself to lifelong professional development.

Although the book is not a traditional "training" book, it still
focuses on what makes a successful trainer. It takes a successful
trainer to produce successful training.

Target Audience

10 Steps to Succcessful Training should be read by anyone who holds one of the many roles under the big umbrella called "trainer"—especially if you have been in the business five years or less. So whether you are a career coach, competency expert, computer-based training designer, continuous-learning coach, corporate trainer, courseware designer, curriculum development specialist, employee development specialist, facilitator, instructional designer, instructional technologist, instructor, knowledge manager, leadership trainer, multimedia engineer, performance analyst, talent development trainer, technical trainer, training leader, or workforce diversity director, there is probably something in the book for you.

I purposefully listed the various roles to demonstrate how broad the training profession has become over the past few years. The list appears to be quite diverse, but all of these roles play an important part in ensuring that the individuals we work with gain knowledge and skills to improve their performance and to meet specific organizational goals.

Often the book addresses the generic term "training" whether offered in a classroom or through some electronic means. However, because classroom training continues to be the most used delivery method, hovering around 70 percent of all training delivered, several steps have more of a classroom focus. Computer-based training (no instructor) and instructor-led training from a remote site (via web conferencing or videoconferencing) have each grown slightly over the past several years. Therefore, you will also find specific content that addresses technology alone; for example, Step 4 offers tips for planning and preparing for a webinar. So as you can see, there is something for everyone in *10 Steps to Successful Training*.

Format of the Book

10 Steps to Successful Training is presented in 10 steps, not chapters. You may wish to read the book from front cover to back, although it is not necessary. Each of the steps provides a stand-alone reading section. You could turn to just one of the steps and read it in its entirety without reading the rest of the book to learn what the step offers.

The book has been formatted to address the purpose of this series—to save you time while providing instruction. Each step is formatted and presented in exactly the same way with an overview of the step's key topics listed on the first page.

Within each of the steps you may find worksheets, templates, checklists, summary sheets, evaluations, examples, and step-by-step instructions to assist you in implementing the content within each step.

Each step ends with three to five Personal Steps to Success. These suggestions can help you put into action the concepts described in each of the 10 Steps. They truly are your personal steps to success.

In addition, sprinkled throughout each step, you will find several Pointers. Pointers are quick ideas or reminders that will help you remember the concepts or suggest ways that you can do something to implement the content immediately.

Organization of the Steps

10 Steps to Successful Training is presented in steps that are loosely organized in the order in which one might think of them. I say "might" because there is no one correct order. If you were following an instructional systems design model (which you are not), you would most likely attend to these steps in this general sequence.

In addition, the steps have not been placed in priority order. If they had been, I definitely would have presented Step 10, which addresses lifelong professional development first, because I believe

that is the most important one of all. As the book unfolded, however, it seemed that the topic was positioned best as the last step.
Maybe it's a situation of "saving the best 'til last."

Let me share a brief overview of each of the steps.

◆ **Step 1: Understand the Role of the Trainer.** Every
trainer needs to understand the valuable research that
has gone before to provide a rationale for why we do
what we do. This means we are less likely to skip important elements of training that make a big difference in how our participants learn best.

◆ **Step 2: Align Training to Improve Your Organization's Bottom Line.** This step addresses the very reason we are all in business—to make a difference. It's
the bottom line. This step is important for success because your organization expects a return on its investment in training.

◆ **Step 3: Use Adult Learning Principles to Design and
Deliver Training.** Many trainers can list the assumptions of adult learning theory, but do not always follow their own advice to implement the assumptions.
This step is critical to successful training because it is
the foundation upon which all training should be
built. Without it, training will be a wasted effort.

◆ **Step 4: Prepare to Succeed and Be Credible.** In our
busy, fast-paced world it is almost impossible to find
adequate time to prepare. Yet prepare we must. Preparation is one of the few elements of training over
which all trainers have complete control. Inadequate
preparation can render a training session close to useless. The waste of time and money and reduction in
participants' confidence and reliance in training make
this the reason this step was chosen as one of the
steps to success.

◆ **Step 5: Create a Safe and Engaging Learning Environment.** This step is important for success because it

helps trainers understand what might prevent a participant from getting involved. Related to Step 1, it is a prime example of turning research into a practical application. Understanding how to establish conditions to ensure successful training is key. Remember, it's all about the participant.

- **Step 6: Facilitate Effectively—Learning Is About Active Engagement.** The training profession, like the rest of the world, is trying to do more in less time. In our profession this translates into removing active learning. Conducting a training session in one hour instead of three is not always the right way to save money. In fact, in some cases, if the hands-on, interactive learning aspect has been removed as a result of time constraints, it is likely that participants have not gained what they needed. Using facilitation skills is important to the success of training to get the job done.

- **Step 7: Present Like a Pro—Presentation Is Key.** The trainer's presentation can make or break a training session. Fair or not, poor presentation techniques get in the way of learning. As an example, think back to your worst college professor and what made him or her so bad. How much did you learn in that class? If your participants aren't learning, your training is failing. Smooth presentations are a prerequisite for successful training.

- **Step 8: Make It Interesting—Use Lively Openings, Transitions, and Powerful Closings.** This step is important for successful training because it ensures that learners' needs are met from beginning to end, without hindering the flow and results of training.

- **Step 9: Don't Forget Classic Techniques That Enhance Learning.** This step provides a potpourri of ideas to save time, increase enthusiasm, and result in learning. The ideas are important because they engage the participants, but they are equally important because they keep trainers excited about what they do. Successful training depends on both of these things.

◆ **Step 10: Get Involved—Helping Others Learn Is Fun and Rewarding.** This step is important because it keeps trainers involved, excited, and knowledgeable about training. We know that training is all about the learner. *But*, it takes an excellent trainer to know how to guarantee that it *is* all about the learner. Successful training depends on successful trainers.

I hope you enjoy reviewing each of these steps as much as I have enjoyed developing them for you. Begin now to take your first of 10 steps to successful training. And don't forget to check out the last page of each step to learn what you can do to quickly implement aspects of each of these critical steps.

Understand the Role of the Trainer

OVERVIEW

> Understanding the vital role of training to the rise of civilization
>
> Identifying key research events that shape today's training
>
> Identifying ways to use history to shape successful training

Let's open this book with what I believe is a major failing for many in the training profession. We often know how to apply best practices, but we don't know where the practice came from; what research might be behind it; or, most important, why the practice is essential.

This chapter will guide you through the history of training and highlight some of the most significant events and the most noteworthy research and theories that have enriched training's role today. It will also help you relate these historical events to what you do and explain how you can use the knowledge to improve the training that you design and deliver.

This Step Is Important for Success

This step to success explores the historical role training has played in getting us to where we are today.

Oh no, not history! That's a typical response because our days are focused on rapid change and the progress of the future. We prefer to delineate our daily activities in terms of where we are heading, not where we have been. The fast pace means that we barely have time to think about the nuances of the future, and certainly no time to think about the outdated information from the past.

However, I believe it is important to find some time to explore the vital role the training vocation has played in the rise of civilization. Examining the past sequence of training efforts helps put the development of the profession in perspective. Understanding these key events provides some underlying pride in what we do. In addition, we must learn from the past to do our best in the future. An indifference to the historical perspective sometimes means that we learn the same lessons all over again.

In addition, exploring more recent research that has shaped training helps us understand why we do some of what we do when designing and delivering training sessions. I have heard it said that, "He who controls the past controls the future." Our knowledge of the history of training shapes the way we understand the present, and therefore, how we can constantly improve in the future.

Understanding the history and events that have shaped the profession is a first step to successful training.

The Earliest History of Training

Depending on how you define "training," you might imagine it started at the beginning of time as early humans passed on how-to tips to each other about everything from the best places to find berries, where to avoid dangerous animals, or even how to start a fire. Where can we start this historical perspective to provide you with the insight you need? Let's take a quick trip down the history highway. You may be surprised at how early some of the events that shape our work today occurred.

This section addresses the time period starting about 3500 BC and takes us from antiquity through the Middle Ages. Like most things, training made a far-reaching transformation during the Industrial Revolution and that is where we will divide this short history lesson.

Training History Timeline

- **3500 BC:** The ancient city of Kish in Sumer was built using consistent brick-laying techniques. The work was performed using an apprenticeship system in which knowledge was transferred from one person to another, or from one person to many people. In addition to the skills passed on by artisans, ancient temples taught religion and art; armies trained soldiers; and apprenticeship was the process of instruction in medicine, law, and other occupations.

- **2100 BC:** Guidelines for governing apprenticeships were instituted in the code of Hammurabi, who placed a set of laws in the temple of Shamash (God of Justice) in Babylon.

- **500 BC:** One of the first action-learning philosophies is credited to Lao-Tse, who wrote, "If you tell me, I will listen. If you show me, I will see. But if you let me experience, I will learn."

- **400 BC:** Socrates (470–399 BC) engaged learners by asking questions (using the Socratic or dialectic method), insisting he knew nothing; this technique allowed others to learn by self-generated understanding.

- **385 BC:** Plato (428–348 BC), a student of Socrates, captured the dialogues, which have inspired thinkers for more than over 2000 years; he also founded the first university near Athens.

- **300 BC:** Aristotle (384–322 BC) placed a strong emphasis on balanced development that included play, athletics, music, debate, science, and philosophy. He observed that relationships among ideas facilitated understanding and recall.

- **400–1100:** The Middle Ages saw the growth of the apprenticeship concept. As the knowledge and skills required to use tools became more specialized, parents were unable to teach their children everything they needed to know so they were apprenticed to artisans, who had specialized skills and tools for various trades. Apprentices lived with the artisan and were not paid for their work, because learning the skills of a trade was considered very valuable.

- **900:** The first schools were formed; content was transmitted from teacher to students in a pedagogical way.

- **1300–1600:** Guild associations peaked; it was the guild members who established quality standards for the product and the work process.

- **1800s:** The Prussians used maps, wooden blocks to represent armies, and learner critique (feedback) to train the military. This is one of the earliest examples of gaming.

Training Advances Starting with the Industrial Revolution

Like most industries, training underwent dramatic changes with the onset of the Industrial Revolution. You might say that training had a revolution of its own. Listed here are a few of the facets of learning that changed, the research that led to the changes, and the individuals responsible for these advances in the field of training:

> **POINTER**
>
> Think about how you can implement Aristotle's observations in your training sessions.

- **1824:** An accepted link between education and training occurred when the Rensselaer Polytechnic Institute in Troy, New York, became the first college of engineering, providing courses in engineering, agriculture, business administration, accounting, journalism, and a variety of other fields.

- **1880s:** The case method was developed by Christopher Langdell at Harvard Law School.
- **1910:** The role-play method was introduced by Dr. J.L. Moreno in Vienna, Austria, but became more popular in the 1930s after he moved to the United States.
- **1911:** Frederick Taylor published *The Principles of Scientific Management.* Taylor called his method Scientific Management, which used time and motion studies to find the one best way to accomplish a task.
- **1913:** First introduced by Ford Motor Co., the moving assembly line required special training for the entire work force.
- **1917:** Charles R. Allen adapted J.F. Herbart's pedagogical framework into a model he called the "Show, Tell, Do, and Check" method of job instruction to solve the urgent need to train shipyard workers. His findings, and those of the army during the war, resulted in the development of several training principles, including
  - Industry should use supervisors to conduct training.
  - The optimal group size for training is nine to 11 people.
  - Task analysis should be completed prior to training.
  - Workers develop loyalty when given personal attention during training.
- **1920s:** Two books were published that began to change our understanding of how adults learn—

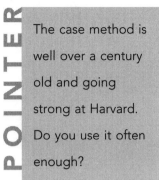

POINTER

The case method is well over a century old and going strong at Harvard. Do you use it often enough?

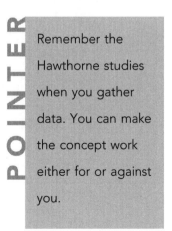

POINTER

Remember the Hawthorne studies when you gather data. You can make the concept work either for or against you.

POINTER

The Significant and Unexpected Hawthorne Study Results

The Hawthorne studies are considered the watershed event for relating behavioral science to training. In 1924 the National Academy of Sciences, in cooperation with the National Research Council, embarked on an experiment to determine the relationship of environmental influences to the efficiency of workers on the job. The research took place at the Western Electric Company's Hawthorne plant near Chicago.

Harvard psychologists, led by Elton Mayo and his associates F.J. Roethlisberger and William J. Dickson, formed experimental employee groups and manipulated workplace conditions such as temperature, light, humidity, and rest periods. They recorded the results to determine how these changes affected the efficiency of the workers.

The researchers found that, almost regardless of what changes were made in the work environment, efficiency increased among the experimental groups of workers. This produced what is known today as the Hawthorne effect, the theory that employees will perform more efficiently simply because they are given special attention.

In addition to the findings of the original premise that physical conditions in the workplace will affect efficiency, other unexpected findings were even more significant. Some of these influences affected efficiency and productivity much more strongly than did the working conditions. For example, employees were more productive when working in groups than when working in isolation. They also found that wage incentives alone did not improve production and that workers would sacrifice greater productivity for group acceptance.

The interviewing program demonstrated that complaints are often symptoms of underlying problems because employees can't always state—or even recognize—what the real problem is without the assistance of someone whom they believe will understand them. This is significant as it helps supervisors understand their important role in encouraging communication with employees.

The study was initially expected to be relatively brief, but actually lasted almost 10 years; it ran until 1933 because of its unexpected and significant results. Ultimately, the researchers concluded that employees' behaviors are usually determined by a complex system of related factors. All of these factors should be considered before determining improvements and predicting outcomes—true systems thinking.

Source: Miller, Vincent, *The Pfeiffer Training Annual*, 2008, Biech, ed., Pfeiffer, San Francisco, pages 110–111.

Thorndike's *Adult Learning* and Lindeman's *The Meaning of Adult Education.*

◆ **1924:** Sidney L. Pressey created a crude teaching machine suitable for rote-and-drill learning.

◆ **1924–1932:** The Hawthorne Studies, conducted by Western Electric Company and lead by Elton Mayo (Harvard), and his associates F.J. Roethlisberger and William J. Dickson, demonstrated that individual behaviors may be altered because people know they are being studied. These social dynamic work environment concepts have had more of a lasting influence than most research. See the pointer: The Significant and Unexpected Hawthorne Study Results for more information.

◆ **1932:** Rensis Likert presented the Likert Scales, used to measure attitude in surveys, providing a range of answers from "strongly disagree" to "strongly agree."

◆ **1940s:** John Dewey, considered to be the leading progressive educator of the 20th century, emphasized practical ideas and hands-on learning and opposed authoritarian methods in teaching. His ideas prompted a drastic change in the United States' education system.

◆ **1950s:** European educators started using the term "andragogy," from the Greek word "anere," for adult, and "agogus," the art and science of helping students to learn.

◆ **1941–1945:** World War II created a need for a fast and efficient training method. Training Within Industry (TWI), an advisory service formed by the National Defense Advisory Commission, developed the systematic on-the-job training method called JIT (Job Instructor Training). Its goal was to train supervisors in defense plants how to instruct their workers in as short a time as possible. This is the birth of both the train-the-trainer and just-in-time training.

◆ **1940s:** The TWI trainers became more aware of the importance of the use of audiovisuals and introduced tools such as training films, filmstrips, slides, simulators, flipcharts, flannel boards, and models.

- **1940s:** Today's job-performance aid started as a printed card that contained step-by-step instructions on performing a specific task. Workers did not have to memorize the steps. This alternative is one of the first examples of improving job performance.

- **1942:** The American Society of Training Directors (ASTD) was formed at a meeting of the American Petroleum Institute Committee on Training in New Orleans, Louisiana.

- **1943:** Abraham Maslow published "A Theory of Human Motivation" in the *Psychological Review Journal.* This motivational model, or as we know it today "Maslow's Hierarchy of Needs" presents the idea that a higher need, such as self-actualization, is recognized only after lower needs are fulfilled.

- **1946:** Kurt Lewin (1890–1947) launched the Research Center for Group Dynamics at the Massachusetts Institute of Technology. He is known as the father of organization development for his many contributions in change theory, action research, action learning, force field analysis, and group dynamics. Today's experiential learning took root in his learning cycle of action, reflection, generalization, and testing.

- **1950s:** The military developed instructional systems design (ISD), a systems approach to integrating all the components from start to finish of developing and delivering training. The term *task analysis* was used by the Air Force in the early 1950s to refer to procedures for anticipating the job requirements of new equipment under development.

- **1956:** Benjamin Bloom published *Taxonomy of Educational Objectives*, identifying three learning domains: cognitive (knowledge), psychomotor (skills), and affective (attitude). This is the beginning of the KSAs as we

> **POINTER**
>
> There is much to learn about Kurt Lewin. If you are not familiar with his name and his work, I highly suggest you learn more.

know them today. A lesser known fact about Bloom is that he recommended instructional techniques that varied both instruction and time according to learner requirements. This gives instructional designers the motivation to individualize learning, matching the learner to the material and training methods.

◆ **1959:** Don Kirkpatrick introduced measurement into training requirements with his four-level model of evaluating training: reaction, learning, behavior, and results.

◆ **1959:** Frederick Herzberg developed a list of factors that affect employee satisfaction. Although the list is similar to Maslow's Hierarchy of Needs, it is more closely related to work. Hygiene factors (dissatisfiers) such as salary, job security, working conditions, and supervision, must be present in the job before motivators (satisfiers) such as recognition, advancement, growth, and job challenge can be used to stimulate employees.

◆ **1962:** Robert Glaser introduced the concept of instructional design and advocated individually prescribed instruction (IPI), in which the results of a learner's test scores are used to plan individual training. Glaser is also believed to be the first to use the term *criterion-referenced measures,* which measures results against the learner's ability to meet specified objectives (criterion) once training has been completed.

◆ **1962:** Robert Mager published *Preparing Instructional Objectives,* which furthered the criterion-referenced measurement concept. An objective describes in measurable terms who will do what, under what conditions, and to what degree of success. Objectives incorporate the task (behavior), condition, and standard (or measure of success).

◆ **1962:** Robert Gagné published *Military Training and Principles of Learning,* which demonstrated a differentiation of levels of learning in psychomotor skills, verbal information, intellectual skills, cognitive strategies, and attitudes. His work complements Bloom's *Taxonomy.* He is most well known for his nine instructional events *(The Conditions of Learning and the Theory of Instruction,* 1965), which identify conditions required for learning to occur. We still rely on these nine conditions:

- gain learners' attention
- share the objectives
- stimulate recall
- deliver content
- use methods to enhance understanding, for example, provide guidance, state relevance
- provide practice opportunities
- provide feedback on performance
- assess performance
- enhance retention and transfer to the job.

POINTER

You probably know the importance of Gagné's conditions of learning. Therefore, you may wish to read more about this topic to enhance your knowledge of this key research.

- **1973:** Considered the father of adult learning theory, Malcolm Knowles published *The Adult Learner: A Neglected Species* and started to popularize the concept of andragogy, a set of assumptions that characterize adult learners (see Table 1.1). This list changed in number and in scope as Knowles perfected his theory. Knowles and others identified characteristics comparing andragogy to pedagogy (see Table 1.2).
- **1975:** Florida State University developed the ADDIE model (analysis, design, development, implementation, and evaluation). There are several ISD versions with an unlimited number of flavors, the ADDIE model is probably the most popular.
- **1981:** Patricia Cross's book, *Adults as Learners,* introduces three features of lifelong learning: a holistic concept of growth and learning, a wider view of delivery (who and where), and the self-direction of the learner for life.
- **1984:** David Kolb's *Experiential Learning: Experience as the Source of Learning and Development* theorized that people develop preferences for different learning styles. Kolb's model is built on the idea that learning preferences can be

STEP

TABLE 1.1
Malcolm Knowles's Adult Learning Theory Assumptions

Malcolm Knowles, father of adult learning theory, took the topic of adult learning from theory to practice with his adult learning theory assumptions:

◆ Adults have a need to know why they should learn something before investing time in a learning event.

◆ Adults enter any learning situation with an image of themselves as self-directing, responsible grown-ups.

◆ Adults come to a learning opportunity with a wealth of experience and a great deal to contribute.

◆ Adults have a strong readiness to learn those things that will help them cope with daily life effectively.

◆ Adults are willing to devote energy to learning those things that they believe will help them perform a task or solve a problem.

◆ Adults are more responsive to internal motivators, such as increased self-esteem, than to external motivators, such as higher salaries.

Source: Biech, *Training for Dummies*, 2005.

described using two continuums: active experimentation–reflective observation and abstract conceptualization–concrete experience. The result is four types of learners: converger (active experimentation–abstract conceptualization), accommodator (active experimentation–concrete experience), assimilator (reflective observation–abstract conceptualization), and diverger (reflective observation–concrete experience).

◆ **1990s:** PLATO, the first computer-based training system, was built in 1959. However, computer-based training was little more than programmed teaching machines until PLATO (Programmed Logic for Automated Teaching Operations) evolved into its current version.

◆ **2006:** The ASTD Certification Institute formally launches its individual certification program.

We've come a long way to ensure that training is successful. Yes, there are other names and theories that I might have included in

TABLE 1.2
Comparing Andragogy with Pedagogy

Andragogy	Pedagogy
Learners are known as "participants" or "learners"	Learners are known as "students"
Belief that participants have an independent learning style	Belief that participants have a dependent learning style
Objectives are flexible and can be customized for individuals and the group	Objectives are predetermined and inflexible
Assume that learners have experience to contribute	Assume that learners are inexperienced and/or uninformed
Active training methods, e.g., case studies, role plays, are used	Passive training methods, e.g., lectures, are used
Learners influence timing and pace	Trainer controls timing and pace
Participant involvement is vital to success	Participants contribute little to the experience
Learning is real-life-problem centered	Learning is content centered
Participants are seen as the primary resources for examples and solutions	Trainer is seen as the primary resource who provides answers, examples, and solutions

this list of key research and events that shaped today's training, but I believe we've covered the highlights.

It is interesting to note how many of the events from both the very early history of civilization through the present influence the work that trainers do every day. It is equally important to not only apply best practices in training, but to understand the theory behind the practice.

The next section will help you ponder implementation methods to ensure you have more successful training sessions.

How to Use History to Shape Successful Training

A simplified history lesson displays how training events, theories, models, and research have built on each other to evolve into training as we know it today. It is noteworthy that many of the practices from decades ago are still significant in successful training. For example:

♦ Although we have added Phillips's ROI (return-on-investment), Kirkpatrick's four levels of evaluation continue to be the basis for good training measurement.

♦ The works of Bloom, Glaser, and Mager still guide the best way to write learning objectives.

♦ Gagné's nine conditions of learning are practiced in classrooms and on e-learning events all over the world.

♦ Even if we are designing a podcast we still rely on Knowles's assumptions about the adult learner.

♦ Maslow's Hierarchy of Needs constitutes much of what we consider "human nature" during these changing times.

POINTER

Use the Worksheet as a discussion guide the next time you deliver a train-the-trainer session. Have participants identify the specific actions they will take to make their next training sessions a success.

These are general examples. The significant role of history truly comes to life when you relate these events and their significance to what you do. It becomes even more powerful when you identify ways to use history to increase the level of training success in your work. Use Worksheet 1.1 to help you incorporate the historical aspects of training into your own development as a trainer. Continue to learn more about the principles and theories of training. It will make you a more valuable asset to your organization and your participants.

Personal Steps to Success

These steps will add to your training knowledge base.

1. For a more in-depth discussion of the history of the profession, read "The Evolution of the Training Profession" by Tora Estep, the first chapter in the *ASTD Handbook for Workplace Learning Professionals,* then put more of what you learned into practice.

2. Malcolm Knowles stated that "Most of us only know how to be taught, we haven't learned how to learn." Think about this statement and jot notes about

    ◆ how this statement relates to you personally

    ◆ how this statement relates to you as a trainer

    ◆ how this statement relates to your learners.

3. Once you've completed Worksheet 1.1, schedule a meeting with your supervisor to discuss the changes you would like to make based on what you've learned.

WORKSHEET 1.1

Exploring Historical Significance for Successful Training

Historical Event	Demonstrated Principle	Significance	Rating Myself	How I Will Apply to Ensure Successful Training
1917: Show, Tell, Do, and Check	Supervisors should conduct training	Important to have the right people involved		
1924: Hawthorne Studies	No one factor affects employees	Important to take a systems approach		
1940: John Dewey influence	Use practical ideas and hands-on learning	Relate the training and allow practice time		
1942: ASTD was formed	Trainers wanted to exchange ideas	Network with others in the profession		
1943: Maslow's Hierarchy of Needs	Motivation must be matched to needs	Motivation must aim where the person is		
1956: Bloom's Taxonomy	Objectives must match desired performance	Take time to analyze exactly what learner needs to know or do		

Historical Event	Demonstrated Principle	Significance	Rating Myself	How I Will Apply to Ensure Successful Training
1959: Kirkpatrick's four evaluation levels	Evaluation is critical from several perspectives	Gather data at all levels		
1962: Glaser's individual prescribed instruction	Learners' test scores used to plan individual training	Take learners from where they are to where need to be		
1962: Mager's criterion-referenced objectives	Well-written objectives are vital to training success	Clearly define objectives early in the process		
1973: Malcolm Knowles's andragogy	Adult learner characteristics lead the way to success	Apply adult learning theory to ensure optimum results		

NOTES

_____

_____

_____

_____

_____

_____

_____

_____

_____

_____

_____

_____

_____

_____

_____

_____

_____

_____

_____

_____

_____

Align Training to Improve Your Organization's Bottom Line

OVERVIEW

Linking training to the
business goal

Designing to meet
business requirements

Ensuring follow-up and
application

You probably expect to see an ISD (instructional systems design) model, a training cycle, or at least ADDIE (analysis, design, development, implementation, and evaluation) mentioned. Well it's here—in the background. Think of this book as a movie. In a movie the setting is important to the story line. Let's face it, *Brokeback Mountain* had a good story line, but it just wouldn't be the same if it was set in New York City. You don't usually go to movies to see the scenery or the movie set. You go because your want a good story, which means engaging content. Just as the scenery sets the mood for a movie, imagine that ADDIE sets the stage for this book. It is there in the background; it is important to the 10 Steps, but it isn't the story line of this book. Assume that we just panned the ADDIE scenery, and it's there in the background influencing the next nine steps.

POINTER

Obtain a copy of your organization's strategic plan and business plan. Read through them and tie what you do to these two plans. Identify your contribution to the organization's success. As a second step, obtain copies for your training colleagues and create a dialogue at your next staff meeting about how your department contributes to the organization's success.

Even though we are not following a training cycle in this book, we will address the *10 Steps to Successful Training* in order. Therefore, it's never too soon to remind trainers that their success depends on the success of the business for which they work: Training goals should be aligned with organizational requirements and goals. This step serves as that reminder. What business goal does your training address? This should be one of the first things you consider when you begin a new training project.

Step 2 addresses how to link training and development to the business goal, how to design training and development to meet business requirements, and how to ensure follow-up and application of new skills.

This Step Is Important for Success

Training is not just something that is nice to do. It is a critical part of business. Organizations support training departments so that the departments can do their part to help the organization reach its business goals and objectives. Like any other aspect of business— research, marketing, sales, manufacturing—training requires an investment. Organizations also expect a return on their investment. When training is the investment, the organization expects a return in terms of improved customer satisfaction, higher sales, improved productivity, an overall increase in the bottom line, or better regulation compliance.

This step is important because your organization expects a return on its investment in training. The better you have tied the training delivered to your organization's goals, the more successful you will be as a trainer. Aligning all training to organizational requirements is the underlying reason why trainers are on the payroll, making this an essential step to successful training.

Linking Training to the Business Goal

To ensure that training is aligned to organizational requirements when designing, buying, or delivering a training program, you need to identify the business goal that the training supports. Think about the kind of goal it is with regard to the business. Goals typically fall into a few general categories: expense reduction, revenue generation, or regulation compliance. Examples of each include

◆ **Expense reduction**: Refresher courses might be required to decrease errors or rework; new information might be used to reduce reliance on more expensive support from consultants or other organizations; new information might also be aimed at increasing employee productivity.

◆ **Revenue generation**: Sales training is usually aimed at increasing sales; customer satisfaction courses are aimed at ensuring customers return and recommend products or services to others.

◆ **Regulation compliance**: Government or industry might require organizations to provide courses to prevent errors as well as fines from regulatory agencies.

Always know how the training program you will deliver addresses organizational requirements. You need to know what training your organization needs. And at times you need to know what training your organization does not need. How can that be? I can think of at least two scenarios.

Sometimes management asks for training when in fact training isn't the solution. For example, if one of your organization's goals is to increase customer satisfaction, no amount of training provided to your customer service department is going to achieve the goal if the real problem is slow delivery of product from your supplier. Even if training is part of the solution, it is rarely the entire solution. Most goal accomplishments require a systems approach—that is, examining the entire set of inputs (material, people, equipment, process, and environment) and aligning them with the goal.

A second scenario occurs when the organization cannot support the training that is requested. If your organization has decided to invest in supervisory training for a large number of people, but does not have positions for all of them, the participants may become frustrated about not being able to use their skills and will find positions in other organizations. Another example occurs when an organization overdesigns training. That is, it designs training that is more expensive, more involved, more time consuming, and more complex than necessary and stops the program before it is completed.

POINTER

Read *The Six Disciplines of Breakthrough Learning: How to Turn Training and Development Into Business Results* by Cal Wick, Roy Pollock, Andrew Jefferson, and Richard Flanagan. This book provides a six-step model that aligns training to business goals.

Your job in all of these situations is to educate management and to provide data that supports your rationale (read needs assessment and analysis).

How can you ensure that training links to the organizational goal?

◆ Review all relevant documentation such as the corporate strategic and business plans, and if the training is linked to a specific department, the departmental business plans.

- Interview leaders of the departments that have requested training to clarify the problem they are trying to solve.
- Discuss the training programs you and your colleagues deliver to ensure the programs are aligned to and support an organizational requirement.
- Be sure to stay abreast of the changes your organization is facing and anticipate the kind of support it will need.
- Use questions like those in Table 2.1 to be certain that you have considered the issues of linking training to organizational goals.

Designing to Meet Business Requirements

A trainer must incorporate myriad items when designing training, including developing objectives; developing materials, instructional methods, timing, and participation; addressing questions; assessing session length and cost; developing audiovisuals and experiential learning activities; creating a safe learning environment; practicing delivery skills; and many others. We can understand your concern about adding yet another thing to remember!

Don't think of this aspect of design as one more thing to remember. Instead, think of it as a process that ties everything together so you can systematically design a holistic learning experience. Think in terms of expanding the learning experience. To meet business requirements, the design doesn't begin when your participants walk in the door and doesn't end when they leave. It begins as soon as you identify who the participants will be and it continues until you are sure participants are contributing to the intended organizational goals.

What can you do to ensure that the design meets business requirements?
- Be sure that your design incorporates steps prior to the learning experience to better prepare participants for what will happen during training. This should include

TABLE 2.1
Questions to Ask Regarding Business Results

Prior to the Training or Learning Event:

◆ What organizational requirement will be addressed with the re-quested training?

◆ What organization or industry issues are driving the training request?

◆ Is training the solution? The only solution?

◆ How will participants' performance improve as a result of the training?

◆ Who are the suppliers and customers who will be affected by the training?

◆ What can the organization expect as a return on its investment?

◆ What is the value of the results?

◆ How will we measure the value?

During the Training Event:

◆ Did the prework and conversations ensure that the participants are prepared as well as they need to be?

◆ Do participants know why they are attending the training session?

◆ How well are participants able to connect what they do to appro-priate business goals?

◆ Do participants know how they contribute to achieving the results?

◆ Are participants confused by mixed messages?

After the Training Event:

◆ Are managers and supervisors involved in the follow-up as planned?

◆ Do participants know where they can receive support?

◆ Was coaching available as necessary?

◆ Are participants held accountable?

◆ Are managers and supervisors held accountable?

◆ How accurate was our measure of value?

a conversation with the employees' supervisors.

- Be sure to clarify with management what the participants are expected to do differently or better and how this aligns to the business goal.
- Identify what actions management will take to support changes following the training session (including reinforcement and feedback) and share these actions with participants.
- Design support—both hard copy and online materials—that can be used following the training session.
- Ensure that participants know how their efforts will affect business goals.
- Be certain that participants know what is expected of them and how they will be held accountable following the training event.
- Clearly identify the trainer's role in support and follow-up.
- Be sure participants know how they can find assistance following the training session.

STEP 2

POINTER

Management's support is critical to ensure implementation of the concepts learned in any training session. Determine what you will need to do to obtain more buy-in and involvement from managers before and after a training experience. What do you want them to do? How can you motivate them? What information can you provide? What do they need to know? How can you coach them?

Ensuring Follow-Up and Application

Ensuring transfer of learning is possibly one of the most important and most overlooked aspects of producing successful training. Yet

STEP
2

POINTER

As a trainer you have an important role in ensuring that the transfer of knowledge occurs. Check Step 9 for suggestions directed at you.

if you step back and think about it, this is truly where success is defined. Many books have been written about the "did training take?" conundrum. Rather than study why it "doesn't take," let's identify what you can do to ensure it does. What can you do to ensure that follow-up and application of the skills and knowledge learned in the training session are implemented?

◆ Follow up with the managers and supervisors within 24 hours of the training session to answer questions or to prod them into action if necessary.

◆ Follow up with participants asking what on-the-job actions they have taken since the training session.

◆ Review the accountability plan put in place during the design process.

◆ Gather data about how many participants are using the support systems (online, coaching, supervisory, and so forth) established for them during the design. Use the data to make improvements where necessary.

◆ Review the training department's role to determine the level of support that is provided and whether it is appropriate for your organization's culture.

Remember that your organization invests in training and developing its people. Therefore, training and development should be treated like other investments—goals need to be aligned, appropriate plans made, and accountability measured.

Personal Steps to Success

1. Use the list of "Questions to Ask Regarding Business Results" in Table 2.1 to prepare for the next training

program you are asked to design or deliver. Share your responses with your supervisor to identify ways that the program might be improved and better tied to your organization's business goals and objectives.

2. Buy copies of *The Six Disciplines of Breakthrough Learning: How to Turn Training and Development Into Business Results* for each of the trainers in your area. Have everyone read and discuss ideas that could be incorporated into your training department's design-and-delivery process.

POINTER

Read *Execution: The Discipline of Getting Things Done* by Larry Bossidy and Ram Charan to identify quotes and support for this important aspect of transferring skills and knowledge.

STEP **2**

3. Before your next training session, meet with the participants' supervisors. Ask them to identify the learning transfer objectives. What do they want their employees to do after returning from the session? Write the actions down word for word. Once you return to your office, send an email to the supervisors you interviewed, thanking them for their time. List the learning transfer objectives in your email and ask for confirmation. Use this information during the training session to help your participants understand the expectations on returning to their workspace.

4. Establish a plan to follow up with participants two to four months after a training session to identify how successful the transfer of learning was as well as any barriers that prevented it from occurring. Use the data to determine improvements that are required in your department and throughout the organization.

NOTES

_____

_____

_____

_____

_____

_____

_____

_____

_____

_____

_____

_____

_____

_____

_____

_____

_____

_____

_____

_____

_____

_____

Use Adult Learning Principles to Design and Deliver Training

Step 1 reminded you of the important role Malcolm Knowles played in the development of successful training. He was adamant about stating the important considerations for adult learning.

Think about yourself. What have you learned in the past month or so? Did you learn the basics of Pilates? Did you find a low-calorie treat at your favorite coffee shop? Did you learn conversational Italian? Did you learn a new way to pay a parking ticket?

Adults learn because they **want** or **need** to learn. Maybe you wanted to learn the basics of Pilates to reinvigorate your desire for exercise. Perhaps you wanted to identify a low-calorie treat to keep your weight down because summer is on its way. Maybe you wanted to learn Italian because you are going to visit Tuscany next spring. Chances are, however, that you didn't necessarily **want** to learn how to pay a parking ticket. You probably received a parking ticket and **needed** to learn how to pay it.

Whether you learned because you wanted to or needed to, this step will help you understand what motivates adults to learn. It will show you what you can do to integrate adult learning theory into both the design and the delivery of your training programs.

This Step Is Important for Success

Trainers are most successful when they provide optimum learning requirements for adults. For many years most teaching was based on a didactic model, which is a synonym for lecture. This model is content centric and led by a teacher. "Pedagogy " is a term that describes this teaching model; it means the art and science of teaching children. Pedagogy refers to a model in which the teacher is in charge and responsible for all aspects of learning.

As we noted at the beginning of this step, most adults learn things because they want or need to. Children do too; however, a child's formal learning is usually led by a teacher and is based on what the child needs to understand to learn something else. That is, children learn to say their ABCs by rote, so that they can write the complete alphabet in kindergarten, so that they can read words and short stories in first grade, so that they can read novels in junior high, so that they can write term papers in high school, so that they can write a Master's thesis in graduate school.

Consideration of learning styles is important for success. We all proclaim to understand and implement adult learning principles, but some do it better than others. To ensure successful training, we all need to be better at incorporating adult learning theory into every nuance of training design and delivery.

Incorporating adult learning theory into your training design and delivery is one of those underlying steps that must be present, but not overtly observable as a step to successful training.

Review Malcolm Knowles and Andragogy

Malcolm Knowles, father of adult learning theory, took the topic of adult learning from theory to practice with his adult learning theory assumptions, using the word "andragogy" to describe them. He wasn't the first to coin the term, however. During the early 20th century, several European countries, such as Hungary, Poland, and Yugoslavia, used the term "andragogy" to describe assumptions about learning, more particularly, adult learning. Hungarian educators, for example, place teaching and learning within an overall system called "anthropogogy."

Knowles popularized the word "andragogy" as he used it to describe the growing body of knowledge about adult learning. It was Knowles's highly readable book, *The Adult Learner: A Neglected Species*, published in 1973, which took the topic from theoretical to practical.

We presented Knowles's assumptions in Step 1. Let's expand them further here and begin to think about how we can incorporate them into the design and delivery of your training programs.

Knowles believed:
◆ Adults **need to know** why they should learn something before investing time in a learning event. As trainers, we must ensure that the learners know the purpose for training as early as possible. Knowles believed that the first task of the facilitator was to help the learners be aware of their need to know the content. This is in conjunction with Bob Pike's radio station WII-FM or what's in it for me. Participants want to know if they will use this information on the job? Will it be required? Will it make their job easier? Will it actually jeopardize their jobs because the organization may not need as many people? What do they have to change to add this to their skill set? Participants need to know how this information or content is going to affect them and why they should care.

POINTER

Before every training session, know absolutely the WII-FM for your participants.

STEP **3**

◆ Adults enter any learning situation with a **self-concept** of themselves as self-directing, responsible grown-ups. Therefore, as trainers, we must help adults identify their needs and direct their own learning experience. Participants come into the training session with a great deal of responsibility and the knowledge that they may lose something by walking into the classroom. Some are afraid that they might lose their freedom to act as adults. Some believe this as a result of strong memories of grade school, when they were under someone else's direction.

◆ Adults come to a learning opportunity with a wealth of **experience** and a great deal to contribute. Trainers will be more successful if they identify ways to build on and make use of adults' hard-earned experience. By linking new material to learners' existing knowledge, trainers create an influential and relevant learning experience for participants. If some participants already know the information, trainers need to tap into that knowledge and use participants to expound on the concepts for others. If too many learners know the content, trainers must question the needs-assessment process. However, sometimes trainers need to deliver content that contrasts with what participants currently experience. In those cases, trainers must help participants remove or change the old concept to make room for the new. Participants will also bring their habits and biases into the session. Learners will have a wide variety of different experiences, which makes it impossible to design a one-size-fits-all training program.

◆ Adults have a strong **readiness to learn** those things that will help them cope with daily life effectively. Training that relates directly to situations adults face will be viewed as more relevant. Whenever possible, training should be scheduled as closely as possible to the time when the new skills and knowledge are required. It does no good to train participants how to use new software if their computers will not have the software for several weeks.

POINTER

Obtaining participants' expectations or hopes at the beginning of your session will tell you what they want and need to learn.

- ◆ Adults are willing to devote energy to learning those things that they believe will **help them** perform a task or solve a problem. Trainers who determine needs and interests and develop content in response to these needs will be most helpful to adult learners. Find ways to continue to relate the training to real life. Participants will learn new information and new skills if they want or need to learn it. Although adults are willing to "devote energy," few are comfortable sitting for too long. Be sure to take breaks so they can rejuvenate and so they can talk with other participants.

- ◆ Adults are more responsive to internal **motivators** such as increased self-esteem than to external motivators such as higher salaries. Trainers can ensure that this internal motivation is not blocked by barriers such as a poor self-concept or time constraints by creating a safe learning climate. Trainers must also be aware of situations that may prevent participants from feeling motivated to learn, including a fear of failure or the inability to deal positively with change. Trainers need to try to identify what motivates each participant.

Integrating Adult Learning Theory into Your Design and Delivery

Most participants ask themselves questions that address Knowles's six assumptions. Trainers need to know how to answer them—not

WORKSHEET 3.1
Incorporating Adult Learning Principles into My Design

Adult Learning Principle	What I Do Now	How I Will Change
Need to Know		
Learner's Self-Concept		
Learner's Experience		
Readiness to Learn		
Orientation to Learn		
Motivation		

in words, but in actions that occur because of a good training design or training delivery.

What can you do as you design or deliver training that will address these questions and deal with your participants' concerns? Here are a few suggestions. Every one of them is doable and easy to implement.

As you read through the six questions relating to Knowles's assumptions, use Worksheets 3.1 and 3.2 as they relate to one of the

WORKSHEET 3.2
Incorporating Adult Learning Principles in My Delivery

Adult Learning Principle	What I Do Now	How I Will Change
Need to Know		
Learner's Self-Concept		
Learner's Experience		
Readiness to Learn		
Orientation to Learn		
Motivation		

training programs that you are currently designing or delivering. How can you strengthen the program based on suggestions from Knowles and answer the questions that participants will ask.

"Why do I need to know this?" Adults have a need to know why they should learn something before investing time in a learning event.

Design

◆ Allow time at the beginning of the course to address the purpose of the session.

- Build in time to respond to questions about the need to know.
- Be prepared to respond to questions about the organization's ulterior motives.
- Ensure that objectives are clear and directed at what the participants will learn.
- Decide if a listing of expectations is required for the session.
- Design a self-evaluation.

Delivery

- Write the purpose on a flipchart page and post it on the wall.
- Give participants time to vent if necessary.
- Be prepared to respond to comments such as, "My boss should be here."
- Link the content to the participant's jobs and particular issues they may be facing.

"Will I be able to make some decisions, or are you going to re-create my grade school memories?" Adults enter any learning situation with a self-concept of themselves as self-directing, responsible grown-ups.

Design

- If a self-assessment has been designed, be sure to allow time for participants to process their results by themselves or in a small, safe group.
- Avoid words in materials that hearken of "school." For example, do not use these words: students, teachers, workbooks, lessons, education, report

POINTER

Make sure that both your words and your body language show respect for your learners.

card, grade, test, desk, classroom, and other terms that remind participants of their school experience.

◆ Design a bright-ideas board where participants can post names of books or ideas that can help other participants with their unique concerns.

Delivery

◆ Welcome participants with a warm greeting and a cup of coffee.

◆ Announce that participants can get up, move around, get a cup of coffee, or whatever it takes for them to be comfortable.

◆ Make the point that questions are encouraged—all questions.

◆ Allow participants to establish their own ground rules.

POINTER

Use the list of six questions at a staff meeting to remind colleagues about the underlying elements that should be incorporated in all the training you deliver. The list is available in Table 3.1.

STEP 3

"Why am I here? Why is she here? What do they think they can teach me?" Adults come to a learning opportunity with a wealth of experience and a great deal to contribute.

Design

◆ Interview participants prior to designing the session to identify typical participant expertise and experience.

◆ If training involves a change in process, identify ways to allow participants to "let go" of the old and welcome the new. Sometimes writing about the experience or self-guided questions address this concern.

◆ Build in time for discussion.

◆ Design an icebreaker that allows participants to get to know each other and what they have to contribute.

TABLE 3.1
Questions Participants Ask

1. "Why do I need to know this?"

2. "Will I be able to make some decisions or are you going to recreate my grade-school memories?"

3. "Why am I here? Why is she here? What do they think they can teach me?"

4. "How is this going to simplify my life? How will this make my job easier?"

5. "Do I want to learn this? Do I need to learn this?"

6. "Why would I want to learn this? Am I open to this information and if not, why not?"

Delivery
- Allow participants to add to the learning objectives.
- Use teach-backs (participants teaching other participants) as one learning method.
- Allow for differences of opinion.
- If everyone in the session understands the content, move quickly. If most do not understand, repeat this segment. If some know it and some don't, find ways to

tap into the expertise in the room to benefit
everyone.

**"How is this going to simplify my life? How will this make my
job easier?"** Adults have a strong readiness to learn those things
that will help them cope with daily life effectively.

Design

◆ Address issues participants face on the job.
◆ Develop case studies, critical incidents, and role plays
that focus on real daily work issues.
◆ Interview participants before designing a training session to obtain specific examples.

Delivery

◆ Allow time for participants to ask questions about implementation back on the job.
◆ Make yourself available at the breaks, at lunch, and
after the session to discuss unique situations with
individuals.
◆ Establish your own credibility without bragging and
couple this with an I-want-to-help-you attitude.

"Do I want to learn this? Do I need to learn this?" Adults are
willing to devote energy to learning those things that they believe
will help them perform a task or solve a problem.

Design

◆ Build in a problem-solving clinic in which participants
bring up their own problems that need solving.
◆ Allow time in the design for self-reflection so participants can revise their thought process or can adapt
the material to their own situations.
◆ Design experiential learning scenarios that link the material to why a participant might either want or need
to invest the time to learn the content.

Delivery

- ◆ Use yourself as an example and share why you wanted or needed to learn something.
- ◆ Post a "parking lot" to encourage participants to list their questions and add ideas.

"Why would I want to learn this? Am I open to this information and if not, why not?" Adults are more responsive to internal motivators, such as increased self-esteem, than to external motivators, such as higher salaries.

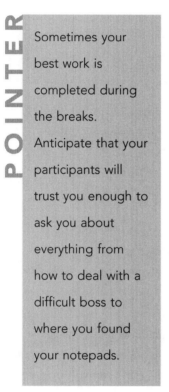

POINTER

Sometimes your best work is completed during the breaks. Anticipate that your participants will trust you enough to ask you about everything from how to deal with a difficult boss to where you found your notepads.

Design

- ◆ Plan activities that help participants explore their own motivation; journal writing or small-group discussions may be useful.
- ◆ Participants can be intrinsically motivated if they know how they fit into the bigger plan, organizationally.
- ◆ Find ways for participants to explore their personal growth and development needs.

Delivery

- ◆ Create a safe learning climate that allows participants to be themselves.
- ◆ Get to know all participants in some one-on-one time.

TABLE 3.2
Tips for Better Design

When designing a training session, ensure that you maximize the learning that occurs. Here are some tips:

◆ build in practical, relevant examples

◆ make the session interactive; learning is not passive

◆ enrich with content; don't underestimate your learners' potential

◆ enhance content with visual and audio support

◆ provide opportunities for practice, repetition, reflection, review, and summary.

As we close this step, remember that Knowles's ideas provide you with the framework for addressing your adult participants' needs. Answering participants' questions to their satisfaction gives you a solid base from which to design and deliver training.

This step to success was all about building that critical base. As you probably know, this isn't all you need to do. Table 3.2 serves as a reminder of the other aspects of design you'll need to keep in mind to create a good training product.

Malcolm Knowles provided us with a great tool. Build a solid base of adult learning theory using his concepts as you design and deliver your next training session.

Personal Steps to Success

1. Read Malcolm Knowles et al., *The Adult Learner: A Neglected Species.* All trainers should be familiar with this easy-to-read book, which changed our work so dramatically.

2. Review your department's current training programs. Make a list of things that could be improved to incorporate more adult learning principles. Share the list with your

supervisor and provide some ideas about how you could begin to address the improvements.

3. Develop your personal adult learning philosophy. Make it about one paragraph long. Identify how you would apply your theory to a training design and/or delivery. How is your philosophy different from Knowles's assumptions? How would your participants respond to your applied philosophy?

4. Although Malcolm Knowles's six assumptions are universally accepted as a brilliant piece of work, they are riddled with duplicate statements and disconnects. If you clarified and simplified them, how many would you have and what would they say?

Prepare to Succeed and Be Credible

OVERVIEW

Preparing the training setting

Preparing the participants

Preparing yourself for a successful training session

Identifying creative ways to practice

I credit Bob Pike for one of the first and most critical lessons I learned as a new trainer. His six Ps for effective training: "Proper preparation and practice prevent poor performance"—have laid a path to successful training for me. There are many reasons why training may not be successful; your lack of preparation should never be one of them.

You are 100 percent in control of what you put into your preparation and practice prior to each training session you design and deliver. That means of course that you must be committed to making the time for preparation. Sometimes it means that you may need to cut into your personal time to be truly "prepared." It may mean that you need to practice with your family and friends. It may mean that you need to stay up late to set up your room for success. It may mean that you need to arise at "O'Dark-thirty" to arrive at the training site to check out audiovisual equipment. It may mean lots of things, and the most important thing that preparation means is that you will be able to "prevent poor performance" and deliver successful training.

This step encompasses preparation from three perspectives: preparing the training setting, preparing the participants, and preparing yourself for a successful training session. The step also identifies numerous ways to practice the content—some you will undoubtedly have used in the past, others might be new and fun to consider using in the future.

This Step Is Important for Success

Participants are involved in your final product—the training session itself. But few even guess how much effort it takes to make the job "look easy." Only those who have been trainers will have a clue as to how much time you have put into your preparation.

Time—investing time is essential. When I first became a trainer I was told to plan on 10 times as much preparation as delivery. That means if you plan to deliver a two-day training session of seven hours each, you need to allow for 140 hours of preparation and practice. That is often impossible in today's fast-paced, changing world. I am not certain if anyone measures this any longer, but I would guess that we are down to a five-to-one ratio, and that is about how much time I invest in each session—and sometimes the set-up day is very long.

I've been in the business for more than 30 years and during that time I have never figured out how to get around the upfront investment of time. I invest about the same amount of time for each session whether it is my first or my tenth delivery. I know that to be my best, I need to prepare and practice.

Why? Why have I called out preparation and practice as one of ten steps to successful training? The primary reason is that it is one of the most important ways to ensure that your participants get what they came for—an excellent learning experience. After all, that's what training is all about—the participants.

You can have the best training design, the coolest PowerPoint presentation, the best business objectives, and a great transition plan. But if you lose your participants because you don't have the materials you need, the audiovisual team delivers the wrong equipment, or you don't remember what needs to be presented in a certain section, your participants may lose confidence in you and may not learn what they came to learn.

Preparing the Training Setting

Have you ever walked in to a training room 15 minutes before the session started and found the audiovisual people poking out from under a freshly skirted table frantically trying to hook an obstinate computer to an equally stubborn projector? Bumped into the caterer wheeling in the refreshment table? Found facilities people scurrying about adding extra chairs? Noticed boxes stacked in the front of the room and participant materials askew on the tables? And noted a distraught trainer trying to arrange her table in the middle of it all? This is not the way any of us would want to start a first day of training. Yet, it happens all too often.

Establishing an environment that is conducive to learning is a small, but important step to successful training. How can you avoid the scenario described above? I only know one solution. Preparation. This means that you

◆ must begin planning at least a week in advance
◆ may need to get up very early to arrive at the site
◆ may need to stay late at night to get into the room after the dinner group the evening before
◆ will probably need to make special arrangements with the hotel or building's night or morning staff

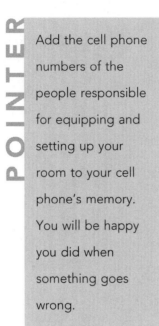

POINTER

Add the cell phone numbers of the people responsible for equipping and setting up your room to your cell phone's memory. You will be happy you did when something goes wrong.

◆ will need to coordinate with a number of people: hotel sales and catering or your company's food service, the audiovisual team, facilities staff, building janitor, or hotel housekeeping

◆ may need to be prepared to rearrange your room upon seeing it (I often do).

Planning and coordination ensure that your participants will arrive to a welcome and relaxed atmosphere. A room that is ready and waiting for them is the first statement of the training session, and it says someone took the time to prepare. Checklist 4.1 presents a list of questions you might ask about the location.

What should participants see for the best learning environment?

✔ **Order:** Boxes are hidden; chairs are aligned to the tables; participant manuals, name cards, and other materials are lying on the table identically at each place setting.

✔ **Seating:** Chairs and tables should be arranged to best meet the session objectives (see Table 4.1) and should be the most comfortable choices available. All participants should be able to see the audiovisuals from their seats.

✔ **Refreshments:** If provided, refreshments should be set at one end of the room on clean table linens and include everything a participant might need.

✔ **Trainer's Table:** This is a table at the front of the room with materials ready to use in the order in which they will be required during the session.

CHECKLIST 4.1
Questions to Ask About the Location

Good preparation means that you have all the answers about the location that you need. Use this checklist prior to your next training session to prevent as many mix-ups as possible.

When?
- ❐ Date of the training?
- ❐ Start and end times?
- ❐ Does the allotted time match what's needed for the content?
- ❐ Time of breaks, lunch?

Where?
- ❐ Where is the session?
- ❐ On site or off?
- ❐ What's the address?
- ❐ Room number?
- ❐ What's the size of the room?
- ❐ Do you need breakout rooms?
- ❐ Is the room readily accessible to all?
- ❐ Is food available nearby for breaks or lunch?
- ❐ Do you need directions? Is it easy to find?
- ❐ What's traffic like?
- ❐ Will participants need to travel to get to the site?
- ❐ Telephone number of the site? _____ What time are the phones covered?
- ❐ Is public transportation available?
- ❐ How do you get materials to the site?
- ❐ Is the room free of obstructions and distractions?
- ❐ Is there enough wall space if you intend to post flipchart pages?
- ❐ How is heating and cooling adjusted—by you or staff? And if staff, who is the contact person?

What?
- ❐ What kind of training is expected?
- ❐ What resources are required?
- ❐ What materials do you need and how do you get them?
- ❐ What audiovisual equipment is required and who supplies it?
- ❐ Will you have a room and group size that will require a microphone? _____If yes, who is the contact person?
- ❐ What is the contact number for the audiovisual setup _____?

Who?
- ❐ Who is the key planner?
- ❐ Who are the participants? How many?
- ❐ Can you get a participant list?
- ❐ What information can you learn about the participants? Background? Positions?
- ❐ Why were you chosen to deliver training?
- ❐ Who is the contact person at the training site? What are this person's work hours? Contact numbers on site and cell? _____

✔ **Audiovisuals:** All equipment must be set up and ready to go. It's nice to have something on the screen, at least the title of the program, so participants know they are in the correct room; another option for the opening screen is a series of rotating quotes that participants can read while they sip their coffee.

✔ **Lighting:** Lighting should be bright and cheery. Natural lighting is best, but if you are in a ballroom without windows, be sure that the facilities staff has turned the lights up to the brightest setting. You should know how to adjust the thermostat if necessary.

✔ **You:** Be ready and waiting to greet participants as they arrive. If you've examined the participant list you might have picked up a few opening discussion items, for example, where they are from, their department, a participant's unique name. You should be prepared at least 30 minutes prior to the session so that you can greet your participants and make them feel welcome on their arrival.

What about table arrangements? The room setting should further enhance your learning environment and will have an impact on your training results. You should select the arrangement that best meets the needs of your training objectives. Is the objective to have participants work in small subgroups most of the time to "build" that team? Is the objective to move participants into lots of different subteams so that they might at one time or another work with everyone else in the room? Is the key objective to strengthen one large team? Will there be lots of small-group work? Large group discussions? Active movement? Do you intend to mix of all of these?

POINTER
Turn the list of what participants should see (as in Checklist 4.1) into your personal checklist of room preparation.

Table 4.1 displays six common seating arrangements and lists the advantages and disadvantages of each.

TABLE 4.1
Six Common Seating Arrangements

Listed below are six of the most common seating styles for classroom training. They are listed in order of my favorite choices from first to last. Often you will not have a choice, and you will need to make do with what you have.

Arrangement	Group Size	Advantages	Disadvantages
U-Shaped	12–22	Encourages large-group discussion; builds the larger team; allows close contact with participants	If a small room, may be difficult to work with those on the other side; linear layout makes eye contact among participants difficult
Chevron (V points to front)	Teams of 4–5 and groups of 16–25	Easy to work in table teams; no one has back totally to back of room; best alternative using rectangular tables	Some difficulty promoting teamwork among the entire group
Rounds	16–50	Promotes teamwork in each cluster; everyone faces the front if chairs on one side only	Difficult to get participation from those who face the back; some participants may need to move chairs to face the front
Single Round/ Square	8–12	Facilitates problem solving; smaller size promotes total involvement; easy for trainer to step out of the action	Media and visual use is difficult; limited group size

(continued on next page)

TABLE 4.1
(continued)

Arrangement	Group Size	Advantages	Disadvantages
Conference	8–12	Allows moderate communication among group	Maintains trainer as lead; creates a sense of formality; inability for trainer to get close to participants
Classroom	Any size	Traditional, may be expected by learners; trainer in control; participants can view visuals	Low involvement; one-way communication; difficult to form small groups

What if you are conducting a webinar or some other e-learning event? Just because you will not be in the same room as your participants, don't think you don't need to prepare. Although each type of technology is different, here are a few ideas for preparation for a webinar:

✔ Select a day and time no less than six weeks prior to the webinar: Research shows that the best days of the week to choose are Tuesday, Wednesday, or Thursday. The best time for a U.S. national audience is between 12:00 and 2:00 p.m. EST.

✔ Send invitations: It appears that email is the best way to invite and inform people of a webinar. Notices in newsletters, links to websites, or press releases are much less effective.

✔ Respond immediately: When participants begin to register for the event, send a response and the guidelines immediately upon receipt. You want to maintain the momentum.

- ✔ If you anticipate first-time users, you may decide to provide an orientation to online learning that includes having them do a systems check the day before; providing written instructions for chatting, posting, and asking questions; demonstrating each tool with an early activity; or even asking a polling question early to get them started.
- ✔ Design your webinar: Plan for a 30- to 60-minute session. Create objectives, and plan your delivery matrix. The maximum number of objectives for this session should be three. Allow time at the end for questions from the participants.
- ✔ Develop a compelling PowerPoint presentation: Make the slides interesting to look at. Use one color scheme and add variety with graphs, clip art, or photos. Dark text on a light background is easier to read; avoid red text completely. Avoid too much text on each slide. Use the 6 x 6 rule (maximum of six words in six lines) just as you would for any other PowerPoint presentation.
- ✔ Keep your PowerPoint file size small: This benefits those who may dial up. One way is to avoid color gradients. Ensure that your slides are 10" by 7.5," sized for an on-screen show.
- ✔ Design to keep participants engaged: Use the interactive web-conferencing features available such as polling, chatting, quizzes, or surveys to keep participants involved. Use the whiteboard feature for brainstorming or creating drawings.
- ✔ Plan for question-and-answer sessions: Prepare for the kinds of questions you anticipate.
- ✔ Practice: Rehearse your presentation several times. Schedule a full dry run with your conference provider to be sure you are comfortable with the platform. Discuss how you will handle problems that may occur.
- ✔ Rehearse the production portion: Include the logistics during your rehearsal, for example, introductions, transitions, handoffs, and the logistics of who will be where.

STEP **4**

✔ During the session, plan to talk into the telephone handset for the best audio quality. A speakerphone or cell phone does not provide optimal quality.

✔ Maintain a studio-like atmosphere: Post a "Do Not Disturb" sign, eliminate background noise, turn cell phones off, mute your computer, close email.

✔ Follow up immediately: Acknowledge all registrants by email. For those who attended send a thank you and instructions for how to access the archive of the event. Send a "sorry we missed you" to any who registered, but did not attend. You may also wish to ask for feedback from all who attended.

These ideas certainly do not cover everything you need to do, but they will get you started along the right path. If you are new to facilitating online you will experience new challenges. For example, two things I find most difficult are managing airtime and not coming across as the expert. I like to facilitate discussion among learners and pull ideas out of them as opposed to "telling." To ensure that this happens, much consideration is required before the session. Activities need to be well thought out and interaction *designed* into the session. You might ask someone you know will attend the webinar to plan to contribute to a certain content area.

Technical difficulties create another challenge, and that's why you will most likely require technical support. The most frequent technical glitch involves participants who have forgotten to get their password or have forgotten how to sign in. You can reduce this challenge by asking everyone to sign in at least 10 minutes before the session begins.

POINTER

You may wish to plant a question in the group to increase other participants' comfort to speak up.

A more personal challenge when running a webinar is getting to know the participants as people. It is difficult, for example, to determine the participants' learning styles or to assist with specific issues and concerns. When listening it is hard to hear the content and even harder to hear the intent of the message.

Even with the obvious challenges, webinars fill a training need. Your preparation and practice is even more critical when using this training option.

STEP 4

Preparing the Participants

Who hasn't assigned a group of participants a chapter or article to read, only to learn when you get to that point that 10 percent have read it thoroughly, 15 percent have skimmed it, 25 percent didn't have time, 25 percent forgot about it, and 25 percent claimed that they never received the assignment? It's happened to most of us.

If you read Step 2 you already know that I believe preparing participants is important for successful results. Here's a list of things I've done in the past that work. You may have others.

✔ Send a welcome letter or email that lists the objectives of the session. Provide a phone number or email address and encourage trainees to contact you with any questions.
✔ Get them involved early in tweaking the agenda by sending them a brief questionnaire that focuses on their unique needs.
✔ Call participants and inform them of the objectives or purpose of the course. Ask if they have anything specific that they might like to cover in the session.

- ✔ Even with the dismal results of assigned reading, you should not be deterred from using it. I have actually had more luck with asking participants to complete an action (rather than read an assignment), for example, ask participants to interview a couple of leaders, survey colleagues, or ask co-workers for feedback.
- ✔ Speak with the participants' managers or supervisors to determine what they want the participants to be able to do when they return. Encourage them to speak with their employees prior to the session. You may wish to include discussion notes for the supervisor to address with the participant.
- ✔ Send an agenda and attach a note telling participants how they can reach you.
- ✔ Send a puzzle, brain teaser, or cartoon that is pertinent to the session and will arouse their curiosity.
- ✔ Send the logistics of the session: location of the site, room number, telephone number for emergencies, plans for lunch, email access, available parking, available public transportation, a roster of other participants, and other pertinent material that will help participants feel comfortable and prepared about attending the session.

POINTER

Review Malcolm Knowles's adult learning principles, as outlined in Step 3, to determine if there is anything that you might be able to do to establish rapport and encourage participants to connect with the content early.

Preparing Yourself for a Successful Training Session

The better prepared you are the more smoothly your session will run and the fewer problems you should encounter. And even when something does go wrong your preparation will pay off because you will be better able to address the difficulty.

Here's my quick checklist of what I do to prepare for the logistics of every training session.

✔ Review the training session thoroughly and list all the logistical details that need to be addressed. Create a checklist of these details and begin to address the items at least a week before the session.

✔ About the same time create a packing list of all the things you need to take with you to the training session. See Checklist 4.2 as an example.

✔ Complete all participant materials and visuals early enough that they can be proofed by someone else and any necessary corrections can be made.

✔ Learn who's in your session to help you customize and plan the focus of your training. You might be able to learn their positions, their understanding of the subject, the reasons they are attending, their opinions, any baggage they may bring with them, or negative concerns you might encounter.

✔ Check on your room about a week before your session. Rooms have a way of rescheduling themselves or double booking with other groups if you do not give them enough attention.

✔ Provide a detailed drawing of how you want the room to be set up. Don't assume, however, that the setup will be correct as a result. I change my room setup more often than not. It seems that if you ask for a room to be set up for 20, facilities people think more is better and will set it up for 25. My problem with this is it appears that there were lots of "no shows."

✔ Begin to make contact with those in charge of the session logistics at least a week in advance to confirm that they have your requests on record. Contact them again the day before the session, reminding them that you intend to arrive either two hours before the session begins, or the night before to check on final logistics. Remind them that you will want your audiovisual equipment set up so that you can try it out ahead

CHECKLIST 4.2
Sample Packing List

Equipment Needs

- ❑ LCD and overhead projector and screen.
- ❑ Place projector on a table with room for supplies, facilitator's guide, and a glass of water.
- ❑ Four flipchart stands with four full pads of paper. One for pre-printed flipcharts and the other kept blank and used spontaneously as needed; two extras for participant presentations on Day 3.
- ❑ Extension cord, extra projector bulb, and an adaptor plug on hand—just in case.

General Materials

- ❑ Markers for trainer
- ❑ Masking tape
- ❑ "Bag It" posters
- ❑ Blank transparencies (one per participant) and pens
- ❑ Trainer's manual
- ❑ Bag of creativity goodies (optional)
- ❑ 100 white index cards
- ❑ PowerPoint presentation

For Each Table

- ❑ Crayons
- ❑ Markers for table tents
- ❑ Role-play cards
- ❑ Sticky notes—colorful, in various sizes
- ❑ Tactile items
- ❑ Large bag of M&M's for prizes
- ❑ Hershey's Kisses or Life Savers for prizes
- ❑ Play-Doh
- ❑ Colored paper, yellow and purple
- ❑ Markers for canvas bags (Sharpies)

For Each Participant

- ❑ Two sizes of different-colored index cards
- ❑ Brown paper bag
- ❑ Envelope
- ❑ Table tent
- ❑ Canvas bag
- ❑ Participant Completion Certificate

STEP 4

of time. Get the name and phone number of the contact person who will be available to let you into the room.

✔ Arrive two hours before the session begins to set up materials, finish last-minute details, tidy the room, rearrange furniture, set up and test equipment, and deal with anything else that crops up.

✔ Because of the possibility of last-minute crises, be sure that you are fully prepared and rehearsed and your materials are in ready-to-go order.

POINTER

Your participants will notice how organized and prepared you are. It's a sign of professionalism. Get organized. Stay organized. See my Procrastinator's Lifeline in Checklist 4.3.

STEP 4

No amount of preparation will avert all problems, but the better prepared you are, the better you will be able to address any trouble that may occur.

Identifying Creative Ways to Practice

Practice makes perfect—or so my grandmother would say. As a trainer you have lots of things to practice. You can start with these:

◆ Use colleagues to practice setting up and debriefing participants on the activities.

◆ Practice the mechanics; for example, using two kinds of audio-visuals at the same time.

◆ Practice the theatrics; for example, if you tell a story with a punch line that needs certain pauses or inflection, know where these belong.

◆ Practice aloud to ensure you have no enunciation problems.

CHECKLIST 4.3
The Procrastinator's Lifeline

Are you a procrastinator like me? Don't have time to read this entire step? Here's a quick and dirty checklist of what you need to do when.

One Week Before

❏ Practice your session in front of a colleague; ask for input, feedback, and ideas.

❏ Know your subject cold. Your confidence will grow if you do.

❏ Memorize the words you intend to use during the first five minutes. The first few minutes are usually the most nerve wracking for a trainer.

❏ Make a list of things you will want to remember to do or pack for the session: equipment; supplies; how to set up the room; what you will place at the participants' seats; names and phone numbers of people who will support the session in any way, for example, the person who has the key to the training room.

❏ If you asked participants to complete a survey or other prework, check to be sure you have all the responses.

❏ Confirm all room arrangements, refreshments, equipment, and supplies.

One Day Before

❏ Run through the entire session, practicing with visuals.

❏ Confirm that you have enough participant materials and all of your supplies.

❏ Check that you have your trainer's guide or notes and keep it with you to take to the session.

❏ Check on everything you need regarding the training site including location of restrooms, refreshments, support staff, and other similar details.

❏ Set up the training room, placing tables and chairs to encourage participation.

❏ Observe the room's mechanics. Will lighting cause any problems? Windows facing east or west? Determine where the light switches are located. Figure out where the thermostat is located and whether you have any control over it.

❏ Set up your equipment, marking placement of the projection table with masking tape on the floor. Test the equipment. Run through PowerPoint slides one last time to ensure they are in order. Practice with the actual equipment. Do you know how to use the wireless remote control? Where is the reverse button? Can you roll the pages on the flipchart smoothly?

- ❏ Arrange the participants' materials on their tables. Place their training manuals, pens, agendas, table tents, markers, and anything else each participant needs neatly at each seat. Place other shared materials they will need for small-group activities or exercises in the center of round tables or equally spaced around a U or other linear placement. These items may include sticky notes, index cards, handouts, or paper.
- ❏ Take one last look around. Empty boxes in the front of the room? Get rid of them. Don't depend on the clean-up crew to discard them for you.
- ❏ Get a good night's sleep.

One to Two Hours Before
- ❏ Arrive at the training site at least one hour before start time.
- ❏ Complete last-minute setup.
- ❏ Organize the space from which you will train.
- ❏ Put your notes in order, turned to the first page, placed where you can stay organized.
- ❏ Ensure visual support is in order, placed where you want it.
- ❏ Fill a glass of water.
- ❏ Add a few paper towels for an emergency.
- ❏ Ensure tools and supplies are where you want them: markers on the flipchart tray, pencil near your notes, sticky notes and index cards at the side, completed table tent at the front of the table.
- ❏ Ensure cords are covered or taped down.
- ❏ Ensure media equipment placement is correct, tested, set to first slide.
- ❏ Make yourself comfortable: Use the restroom, get a drink of water.
- ❏ Move around the room and greet people as they arrive up until two to five minutes before start time.

One Minute Before
- ❏ Take one more peek at your opening line.
- ❏ Take a deep breath.
- ❏ Tell yourself how phenomenal this is going to be.
- ❏ Find a friendly face.
- ❏ Smile.
- ❏ Go for it! There you have it—the long and the short of preparation.

STEP 4

- Practice in the room where you will conduct the training so that you feel comfortable—so comfortable it becomes your room.
- Anticipate questions participants may ask and prepare your responses to them.
- Practice the questions you will ask participants.
- Practice in several different ways:
  - in front of a mirror
  - to your colleagues
  - to your family, friends—even your dog (who will make great eye contact!)
  - with a recorder
  - in front of a videocamera.

Practice and preparation can make your training session all that you had hoped it would be. As Publius Ovidus (43 BC–17 AD) said, "Practice is the best of all instructors."

Personal Steps to Success

1. Create your own checklist for setting up a training room. Create your own checklist for delivering a webinar.
2. Interview supervisors and managers whose employees you train. Ask them for advice about how you might best prepare their employees for training sessions.
3. Start a file of all your checklists, packing lists, and other tools you use to prepare and get organized. You can save time by creating your own lists and prompts that you will use over and over.
4. Put together your own training kit. Include a set of markers, masking tape, pen, scissors, index cards (useful for many things from assessment to evaluation), and other items you use and place them all in a small bag. Your kit will be ready to grab when you need to pack for a training session.

Create a Safe and Engaging Learning Environment

OVERVIEW

Identifying a trainer's responsibility to ensure that adults learn

Discovering ways to create a safe learning environment

Discovering ways to create an engaging learning environment

Thinking back to Step 1, we touched on several theories, models, and practices that addressed the training environment:

- ◆ Charles Allen informed us that workers develop loyalty when given personal attention during training.
- ◆ The Hawthorne Studies concluded that paying attention to people increased their productivity.
- ◆ Maslow's Hierarchy of Needs laid out the five levels of need for all individuals.
- ◆ Malcolm Knowles asserted that adults are responsive to internal motivators and that a trainer must create a safe learning climate.

Step 5 will assist you in determining the best way to create the environment suggested by several training gurus. How do you ensure that participants feel safe—safe enough to ask questions when they don't know and to contribute when they do? How can you create an engaging learning environment—one that makes participants want to learn? How can you ensure that participants feel as comfortable in your training session—whether in a classroom or online—as they do in their normal environments?

This step provides a list of implementation ideas that have worked in various training settings. You will also get the opportunity to determine how you can create a safe and engaging environment for your participants.

This Step Is Important for Success

This is one of those times when you need to pay attention to Abraham Maslow. The five levels of Maslow's Hierarchy of Needs are presented in Figure 5.1. According to Maslow's Hierarchy of Needs, individuals cannot feel the higher needs until those near the bottom are met first. For example, an individual will not have a need for esteem until the first three categories of needs are satisfied.

An understanding of Maslow's hierarchy is important for trainers' success because it helps trainers appreciate what might prevent a participant from getting involved. If you know what affects your learners (review Malcolm Knowles's work), you can predict where participants might be on the Hierarchy of Needs and then adjust when necessary to help them move up the model. Trainers' slight interventions may allow learners to be open to new ideas, to change, and to further their own growth and development. Expectations can be scary and prevent a learner from acquiring the knowledge and skills required. This is a brief chapter, but an important step.

Creating a safe and engaging learning environment is a step you must think about; it does not occur naturally. However, it is a critical requirement for successful training.

FIGURE 5.1
Maslow's Hierarchy of Needs

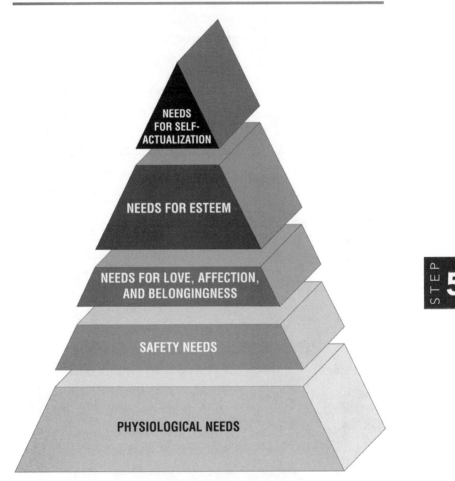

NEEDS FOR SELF-ACTUALIZATION

NEEDS FOR ESTEEM

NEEDS FOR LOVE, AFFECTION, AND BELONGINGNESS

SAFETY NEEDS

PHYSIOLOGICAL NEEDS

STEP 5

A Trainer's Responsibility Is to Ensure That Adults Learn

The burden of learning rests with the trainer. Yes, you will have participants in your sessions who have an attitude and you may believe there is no way to get through to them. You might be surprised. Those who give you the least hope at the beginning often make the greatest turnaround in the end. In addition to all the things you will do in the other steps to ensure that adults learn in your training sessions, you may also

- ensure clear communication
- take into account each participant's learning style
- create a comfortable environment.

Communication always heads the list as a requirement to ensure things work the way they are supposed to work. Communication is always blamed when things don't go as they should. Yet communication almost never gets the stature it deserves when something goes well. Table 5.1 presents a list of potential communication barriers for trainers. The items presented may be barriers for you. Sometimes we become too busy with the work or too relaxed with our communication to consider how our words will be interpreted. A gentle reminder for improvement generally works. Use the list to reassure yourself that communication isn't preventing participants in your training sessions from learning. And if it is, here's the gentle reminder.

Another thing you can do as a trainer is to take into account each participant's learning style. There are several theories available for you to consider:

- David Kolb presents four learning styles: the converger, the diverger, the assimilator, and the accommodator.

POINTER

Maintain a holistic perspective throughout the training session. Don't jump to conclusions about a participant who seems to be uninterested. The individual may have difficulties at home or be concerned about a work issue. Don't overreact, but keep an eye on the situation and take action when it is appropriate.

STEP 5

TABLE 5.1
Barriers to Effective Trainer Communication

Possible Barrier	Rate Your Skill	What You Could Do Better
Jargon and Acronyms		
Language Differences		
Nonverbal Messages		
Visual Aids Outdated		
Nonoperative Visuals		
Boring Presentation		
Assume Participant Knowledge		
Trainer Mannerisms		
Unclear Objectives		
Poor Listening Habits		
Lack of Participant Discussion		

◆ W.E. (Ned) Herrmann professes four brain specializations, each with its own preferred way of learning.

◆ Neurolinguistic programming (NLP) proposes that everyone takes information in through three modalities: visual, auditory, and kinesthetic and that most people use all three modalities.

If most of us take in information through these learning styles, your responsibility to ensure that participants learn means that you need to create an environment that is richly varied.

Because you will have participants with all styles in your training sessions, what can you do? Do what you have been doing all along. Introduce variety to address all the learning styles. For example, create a learning environment that is conducive for the visual learner by

- creating a colorful classroom with colorful paper, various colored materials, index cards, and markers
- showing how to complete the skills using demonstrations, movies, or role plays
- helping participants visualize concepts with graphs or drawings on a flipchart
- using icons to help participants find their way through the materials
- providing written directions when possible
- enhancing content with illustrations, diagrams, props, flowcharts, graphics, and other visuals.

Create a learning environment that is conducive for the auditory learner by

- creating activities that give participants the opportunity to repeat the information aloud
- designing activities that use various small groups, buzz groups, pairs, teach-backs, and discussion groups that permit participants to converse about the information
- using various ways to "tell" the information, including panels, interviews, debates, tapes, and verbal case-study exercises
- providing spoken directions when possible
- avoiding subtle body language or facial expressions to make a point, the auditory learner will miss it.

Create a learning environment that is conducive for the kinesthetic learner by

- creating activities that provide physical action
- providing objects to manipulate and touch; my

favorites are crayons, Play-Doh, Koosh balls, and other tactile toys

◆ encouraging informal breaks
◆ building in time to move around during activities
◆ engaging participants in experiential, hands-on learning activities, including role-playing, scavenger hunts, completing puzzles, making models, relay races, skits, and demonstrations.

POINTER

Know your delivery style. Even if you consider yourself a well-seasoned professional, you need to constantly adjust to take into consideration the various individuals in your session.

Create a comfortable learning environment by considering the mood established in the room. Here are a few thoughts:

◆ Train in rooms that have natural light. When that is not possible, turn the lights on as bright as they can go. Forget about dimming them for your PowerPoint presentations—unless of course there is a spot light shining on the screen. If that is not the case no one should have any trouble reading the slides. If anyone does, shame on you for placing too many words on the slide.
◆ Ensure that the environment looks comfortable. Consider the room yours and the participants your guests. Would you have a stack of empty boxes sitting around if you were going to entertain guests in your living room? How about the broken chair in the corner? The messy stack of furniture in the corner? Clean it up for your guests.
◆ Create enough personal space for everyone—but of course not too much. Your guests should neither be crowded nor need to shout at each other during small-group activities.
◆ Learn how to adjust the lights, the thermostat, the blinds, and the equipment for the participants' comfort.

STEP **5**

- Ensure that you can be heard and your visuals can be seen by everyone in the room; I like to sit in each of the chairs to guarantee that there isn't a problem.
- Provide the most comfortable chairs you can find.
- Remember the small things: coffee, water, extra supplies.
- Allow for plenty of breaks. Breaks are important for physical, mental, and social comfort.

Discovering Ways to Create a Safe Learning Environment

As a trainer, you will encounter every kind of mind-set in your training session. Some participants will view training as punishment for some unknown crime; others will already "know" everything and defy you to teach them. Some will bring the baggage of a bad junior high experience, as if that bad report card arrived yesterday. Still others will bring daily burdens with them, both personal and work-related.

When you prepare to help these folks, remember that your role as a trainer goes much further and deeper than just getting through the content for the day. You have an opportunity to make a difference—a big difference in their lives. On the days that you make a difference to just one person, you will feel the magic and the power of training. Those are the days that are the most rewarding.

Creating a safe haven for learning begins with you. One of the key reasons that you invest so much time in preparation is that you can be certain that the various training elements are aligned and working in concert as best they can. This frees you up to attend to your participants and address their needs.

Create a safe learning environment by
- touching base with participants prior to the session, stating the purpose and objectives of the training session

- greeting participants as they arrive, learning their names, welcoming them to the session, and finding out something about them
- informing participants about the WII-FM (what's in it for me)
- respecting each and every participant—even the difficult ones
- using names and sincere reinforcement
- ensuring confidentiality about what is discussed and what occurs in the training session
- letting them in on who you are—not just your credentials, but who you are as a person.

Discovering Ways to Create an Engaging Learning Environment

If you've paid attention to communication, considered participants' learning styles, arranged a comfortable setting, and created a safe learning environment, you've taken huge strides toward creating an engaging learning environment—one in which learners want to participate and get involved.

Here are just a few more things you can do to create an engaging learning environment:

- Allow the group to contribute ideas about the direction of the session. This participant-driven technique allows participants to take ownership of the session. Yes, you still need to teach the things that are required, but you

POINTER

If participants contribute to and create an expectations list, post it on the wall. As you complete items on the list, check them off. This is good for the participants because they see progress. It's good for you because it keeps you on track.

can usually do that within the expectations of the group. Chances are they will identify topic areas that match the objectives. If not, a bit of subtle direction from you can reshape the expectations. And if presented with a single participant's need, such as a problem with a boss, you can always offer to discuss the topic at break or after the session.

◆ Identify ways that you feel comfortable with to get and keep a group involved. Assuming that you already have a training design that is customized for the group, make sure it is action oriented, experiential, creative, fun, fast paced, varied, and participative. You can always have a couple of quick ideas up your sleeve that boost motivation such as:

  ◆ conducting a pop quiz—for fun and prizes of course
  ◆ seeking opinions and creating controversy within the group
  ◆ entertaining them with a story, a problem, or a lesson learned
  ◆ asking them what they need or want
  ◆ giving them props to use (I like Play-Doh and crayons)
  ◆ challenging them.

◆ Encourage them to ask questions at any time and use a "parking lot" religiously for questions that need to be held.

◆ Watch behavior and behavior changes during the session. If someone was once an active participant and now has pulled away and gone into a shell, you need to check it out. Never hesitate to pull someone aside and ask if you've said or done something that upset the person. Chances are that you have not. It may be a personal issue, a headache, or a boss who continues to leave emergency messages. But you will make an impression on the person that you care. And that is key to creating an environment that is conducive to learning. And in the off chance that you did actually say something that was misconstrued and upset the person, your actions provide an opportunity for you to right the wrong.

Participant engagement and involvement are key to successful training. A huge part of this success centers on the trainer's facilitation skills and the techniques used to encourage participation. The next two steps cover both of these considerations in depth.

POINTER Never confuse enthusiasm with entertainment, funny stories, jokes, or silliness. Enthusiasm is passion for what you do, devotion to whom you do it for, and confidence in how you do it.

Personal Steps to Success

1. Review the work of several of the training gurus mentioned at the beginning of this step and identify what you can do to ensure that you are following their suggestions to create a safe and engaging learning environment.
2. Pose this question to yourself, "If I were a participant in this session, why should I listen to me?" This exercise, done alone, or with several of your colleagues, provides ideas for what should motivate participants to learn. It gives you ideas for what you can do to create an environment conducive to learning.
3. Ask a colleague to observe the first two hours of the next training you conduct to obtain specific feedback on your communication style and how well it creates an environment conducive to learning for participants. Use the communication barriers listed in Table 5.1 as a guide. Use the feedback to make improvements.
4. At your next staff meeting, ask your training colleagues to bring ideas about what they use to create a safe learning environment. Share them in a round robin.

STEP **5**

The Last Word: Enthusiasm

One final thought. Your enthusiasm will take you a long way. You've got to love what you do. You've got to love the participants. You've got to love the materials. And if you don't, you need to look like you do! Your enthusiasm is the secret to the success of this step. Your enthusiasm will be the launching pad for your participants' willingness to listen, to learn, to participate, and to make the desired changes based on the training you deliver. You offer hope, energy, and excitement about the future.

Facilitate Effectively— Learning Is About Active Engagement

OVERVIEW

Defining facilitation

Addressing facilitation's importance

Increasing participation

Facilitators are often on the fence about following the agenda or incorporating what participants desire, about being proactive or responsive, and about presenting content or facilitating discussion. The 2004 American Society for Training & Development (ASTD) Competency Study identifies facilitating learning as one of the key actions required to deliver training. It is described as "adjusting delivery and curriculum to adapt to the audience and the needs of the learners."

This step discusses the importance of facilitation and how to increase participation as one of the best ways to facilitate a learning experience.

This Step Is Important for Success

Training is all about the learner, and an excellent trainer will find ways to involve participants in learning new skills and knowledge.

Knowles has taught us that adult learners want to be involved in learning that will solve their problems and make their daily work easier.

It is not enough for a trainer to "get through" the agenda; trainers must involve participants, which means tapping into facilitative skills.

This step is important for two key reasons. First, training is all about the learner, and facilitation is the way to reach the learner. Second, trainers have been pressured to incorporate more objectives and more knowledge and skills in a shorter and shorter amount of time. The training takes three days? Do it in one! When learning time is compressed, there is a tendency to cut out the activities. When in fact active involvement is the part of training that has the best chance of transferring to the workplace, which is, after all, the whole reason for training.

Understanding the required facilitation role of a trainer and its importance, as well as facilitation techniques such as encouraging participation, is a subtle step to successful training.

Defining Facilitation

Facilitation? Training? Don't facilitators conduct training sessions? Don't trainers facilitate groups? What's the difference? I once conducted a training session with a colleague who was upset with me because I introduced him to our participants as a trainer. He said he was a facilitator, not a trainer.

Even though he wanted a different title, he did the same thing I did. We both designed the event together, we both encouraged participation, we both facilitated discussion, we both conducted small-group activities, and we both ensured that participants would acquire the skills and knowledge our client expected.

Some people get wrapped up in the meaning of words. In this case, I believe a good trainer is a good facilitator who uses facilitation skills. Julius E. Eitington, in *The Winning Trainer*, provides these definitions:

◆ **Trainer:** Term used to describe a learner-centered conductor of a course or program. See also Facilitator (p. 593).

◆ **Facilitator:** A trainer who functions in a way to allow participants to assume responsibility for their own learning. The term is in contrast to the more didactic instructor, teacher, lecturer, presenter, and so on (p. 585).

Eitington believes that the words are interchangeable because the roles are the same. I do as well. Yes, there are facilitators who are not trainers. But there should never be a trainer who is not a facilitator.

But let's not haggle about definitions, let's examine instead why facilitation skills are a critical part of what trainers do.

A "pure" facilitator may never have to present specific content, whereas a trainer may need to do that. So when you start thinking about presenting, what comes to mind? Yep! Lecture! Ooooo that nasty didactic practice! But even a lecture can incorporate facilitative methods to maintain a good model of adult learning techniques. Here are a few suggestions for delivering a facilitative lecture:

◆ Keep the lecture brief, perhaps five to 10 minutes at most. Then change the name from lecture to lecturette. There. Feels better already, doesn't it?

POINTER

Lecterns are excellent barriers to prevent you from interacting with your learners. Don't use them. If they are in your training room, push them out of the way. A low table at your side can hold any amount of notes and supplies you wish and will not serve as a barrier between you and your participants.

- Ask questions to generate involvement throughout the presentations, for example, what do you think happens next?
- Encourage questions from the group throughout.
- Conduct a round robin to get ideas, opinions, or concerns.
- Conduct a poll, for example, how many of you believe that X will be correct?
- Ask participants what they need to learn at the beginning or in the middle.
- Ask participants for ideas or to predict next events or steps.
- Compare or contrast participants' ideas.
- Form buzz groups to consider an idea midway through the lecture.
- Stop midway to ask for a recap.
- Integrate quizzes or puzzles.
- Develop a handout outline of the presentation leaving space for notes.
- Use visuals, graphs, and illustrations to maintain focus.
- Create a conversation, as opposed to a presentation.
- Build in demonstrations or tasks for participants to complete.
- Pass around a model.

Many other methods exist to maintain involvement during a presentation. Check your own roster of ideas. Keep this list handy for the next time you know you need to present new information to participants.

In a few rare instances a straight lecture is required, for example, when laws or regulations must be delivered word for word or when safety is an issue. But for the most part a lecture is not something trainers use very often.

Facilitation Is Important

Why is facilitation an important part of training? We know that it is not enough for trainers to cover all the content; they must allow participants to practice with, experiment with, consider, discover, and explore new information to make it their own. When asked what they wanted most in a trainer or facilitator, participants stated these characteristics:

POINTER

I'll pass this advice to you from someone I respect: A successful trainer is a guide on the side, not a sage on stage.

- ◆ Competence: Someone who demonstrates knowledge of the topic.
- ◆ Organization: Someone who delivers an organized presentation and who maintains organization throughout the seminar.
- ◆ Captivating delivery: Facilitator who grabs and holds participants' attention.
- ◆ Relevance: Facilitator who demonstrates practical applications and uses relevant examples.
- ◆ Responsiveness: Someone who answers questions and addresses individual needs.
- ◆ Enthusiasm: Facilitator who is genuinely excited and interested in the participants and in what is being taught.
- ◆ Participant focus: Someone who involves the audience and encourages participation.
- ◆ Humor: Someone who uses humor to enhance learning and isn't too serious.

STEP 6

Covering all of these may seem like a big task. You might be surprised, however, that many of these skills may be in use at the same time. If you like what you do as a trainer, you may even exhibit these qualities naturally.

The experiential learning process is one way for a trainer to incorporate many of the participants' eight requirements. Besides, the process is one of the best ways for participants to get involved in their learning. Experiential learning activities (ELAs) incorporate five steps:

1. **Experiencing:** completing some defined task.
2. **Publishing:** sharing observations of what happened.
3. **Processing:** interpreting what happened and why.
4. **Generalizing:** relating the experience to real life, the "so what."
5. **Applying:** determining how what was learned can be implemented in the real world.

This list is a powerful tool trainers use to give participants an opportunity to practice with, explore, and incorporate new information. The pointer provides more information about ELAs.

Design your own ELA for a training session you intend to deliver in the future. Follow these guidelines as you design:

◆ Establish clear objectives.
◆ Try the design out with colleagues and get their feedback.
◆ Limit the amount you intend to cover.
◆ Focus on the application: "What will we apply as a result of this activity?"

ELAs are one of the best techniques to use to incorporate adult learning principles.

You will do many things as a trainer that allow you to practice your skills as a facilitator. Here are a few facilitation examples:

◆ Share personal experiences, describe scenarios, or give examples to clarify knowledge.
◆ Create discussion between you and the participants and among participants.
◆ Request ideas and information from participants prior to introducing a new topic.
◆ Facilitate experiential learning activities, case studies, role plays, and games in which the learners discover key information by processing the activity.
◆ Provide opportunities for learners to explore, discover, and evaluate their competencies throughout the training session.

Experiential Learning Activities

Experiential learning activities (ELAs) must meet several common criteria. They generate information that is scrutinized by participants; are highly participative; require processing; and follow a specific, structured process. The five steps in the Pfeiffer and Jones experiential learning cycle, listed here, meet these criteria.

1. **Experiencing: Completing some defined task.**
    Participants are involved in an activity, experiment, game, or some other defined task that produces data and information.

2. **Publishing: Sharing observations of what happened.**
    Participants share their observations and discuss what they experienced, saw, and felt. A facilitator usually starts with a general question and then becomes more specific, allowing participants to express emotions. Questions to facilitate this step might include

    ◆ What happened during the activity?
    ◆ What did you personally experience? See? Feel?

3. **Processing: Interpreting what happened and why.**
    Participants have an opportunity to discuss why something may have occurred and to test hypotheses and rationale in group discussion. Questions for this step might include

    ◆ Why do you think that happened?
    ◆ What did you learn?
    ◆ Based on your experience, what do you think this means?

(continued on next page)

4. **Generalizing: Relating the experience to real life, the "so what."**

Participants explore the "so what" in this step. To ensure that the activity leads to a practical experience, participants identify similar situations based on past experience. Questions to facilitate this step might include

- What situations does this remind you of?
- What does this suggest about . . . ?
- How does what happened help you understand . . . ?
- So what if . . . ?

5. **Applying: Determining how what was learned can be implemented in the real world.**

Participants uncover the reason the experience was conducted and what they can take from it. The facilitator assists them by applying generalizations to real-world experiences. This step answers the "now what" question. Questions to facilitate this step might include

- What will you do differently as a result of this experience?
- How can you apply what you learned back at the workplace?
- How might this help you in the future?
- What's next?

Participants may follow this step with an action plan, keeping a journal, or perhaps discussing the anticipated impact within a small group or in pairs.

- ◆ Facilitate dynamite activities. Here are some guidelines:
- ◆ Arrange participants in small groups before providing the activity instructions. Some participants will have forgotten your instructions while they settle into their group.
- ◆ Be sure to circulate from team to team during the activities. You may be needed to clarify instructions or assist with learning new skills.
- ◆ Watch the time on activities closely.
- ◆ Give time-limit warnings before the time to complete an activity is up: "Wrap up in one minute." "You're about halfway through your time." "You should be in the last half of the exercise now." "You have about five minutes left."
- ◆ Although making sure you have time for everything is important, you still need to make sure you schedule enough breaks. There's no reason to force the group through an activity if no one's listening!
- ◆ Process all activities. Prepare and ask questions that summarize what was learned, identify feelings and thoughts, highlight alternative behaviors, and bring the skills back to the participants' real world.

The common thread running through these ideas is increasing and improving participants' involvement in the process.

Increasing Participation

Encouraging participation is a key part of facilitation and accomplishing your job. The first step in encouraging participation is to build on the safe environment we created in Step 5 and to build trust between the trainer and the participants as well as among participants. Here are some ideas that can get you started quickly:

POINTER

Stick to techniques that are comfortable, building on your strengths.

- Begin to use small breakout groups early in the session to encourage discussion and to overcome any reluctance participants may feel about sharing ideas and concerns with others in the group. I generally create the first small-group breakout during the icebreaker in which participants share something related to the content and themselves, for example, their thoughts about X or their feelings about Y.
- Use participants' names early and often. Use table tents to remind you of who is where. I sometimes keep a diagram of the tables with names, in case a table tent is hidden from view. Using names encourages input and communication.
- Encourage participation with your body language. Good eye contact, nods of encouragement, smiles, and gestures show that you are interested in what the person is saying and that you want more.
- Share something about yourself or laugh about a mistake. This helps to build trust between you and the participants. This reassures participants that you have a human side too and will promote an exchange to build trust.
- Learn and apply techniques to get learners to open up. Some of these include
  - using round robins
  - using index cards to take a poll, ask for opinions, ask for questions, or conduct a midcourse evaluation
  - asking someone else to facilitate a discussion
  - thanking participants for their responses
  - getting even the shyest participants involved, but keeping it easy and nonthreatening.

What are the skills that a trainer requires in the facilitative role to increase participation? Here are some to think about:
- **Communication:** Good communication encourages participation naturally; trainers who are able to listen well, ask questions, encourage questions from participants, accept

STEP 6

input, project assertiveness, and know when to practice silence draw out these skills in others.

- ◆ **Interpretive skills:** Learners need to know that you "get it" to increase their participation level. Trainers must have the ability to interpret participants' nonverbal messages, appreciate their hot buttons, relate to their situations, and correctly determine what they mean.

- ◆ **Interpersonal style:** Trainers display a set of characteristics that allow participants to trust them. These include being willing to share yourself, being people oriented and approachable, being respectful of all opinions, and being organized.

- ◆ **Personal traits:** Traits that encourage participation include a sense of humor, patience, trustworthiness, sincerity, and openness to ideas.

- ◆ **Training techniques:** Participants will be more inclined to participate if you provide clear directions, allow time for processing learning, provide feedback, coach, and provide reinforcement to participants.

- ◆ **Attending skills:** These skills, although a part of communication, go further and show that you care about your participants; attending skills include providing consistent and balanced eye contact, staying engaged, moving around the room during discussions, and providing affirmative nonverbal cues.

POINTER

Some of your participants may be shy. Don't call on them too early in the session. Find a way for them to participate incrementally, for example, in a round robin, or allow them to test an idea in a small group before sharing with the entire group. Sometimes these folks are more analytical and need "thinking" time.

STEP **6**

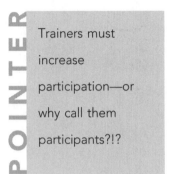

♦ **Process skills:** The way that you encourage and balance participation is also an indicator of the level of participation you desire and includes things such as creating an inclusive environment, balancing participation, encouraging more involvement, and maintaining a flow of interaction.

You can do lots of things to encourage participation. Use Checklist 6.1 to identify other things you can do.

Personal Steps to Success

1. Buy a book about facilitation skills and try a couple of techniques that might be new to you.
2. Develop your own experiential learning activity following the guidelines suggested here, using some of the questions in the experiential learning activities pointer. Submit it to the *Pfeiffer Training Annual* for publication at Pfeifferannual@aol.com.
3. Use the skills in Checklist 6.1 to identify facilitation skills you use regularly and those that you need to reinforce.
4. Join one of the associations for facilitators to gain more experience in this part of your job.

CHECKLIST 6.1
Using Facilitation Skills

You can do many things to ensure that you are using facilitation skills. Here's a list of some of the actions you can take that make a good facilitator. Some of these you have seen in other steps. At the end of your next training session, examine these and determine whether you did each to the best of your ability or whether there is room for improvement. Add a couple of your favorites at the end.

❏ Take time to welcome participants as they arrive.

❏ Create an environment where participants feel comfortable to take risks.

❏ Establish expectations at the beginning of the session.

❏ Elicit specific goals from individuals as well as the more general purposes of the group.

❏ Design a program that allows flexibility to meet participants' needs.

❏ Design experiential activities that encourage discovery.

❏ Encourage questions and answer them to your best ability.

❏ Use "I don't know" when you don't and offer to find the answer.

❏ Be aware of your body language.

❏ Use excellent communication methods.

❏ Remain neutral among participants.

❏ Maintain focus.

❏ Use diplomacy to address differences of opinion.

❏ Correct thoughtfully, tactfully, and gently when a participant is incorrect.

❏ Be considerate and respectful toward all participants.

❏ Maintain a high energy level from beginning to end.

❏ Reinforce freely.

❏ Act as a resource as well as a provider of resources.

❏ Recognize that you are learning along with participants.

❏ Share yourself and your feelings and thoughts in a way that participants can accept or not.

❏ Model compassion for others.

❏ Be positive.

❏

❏

STEP **6**

STEP

6

Present Like a Pro—Presentation Is Key

Attending to what participants hear and see

Staying organized

Managing participants' questions

Even though trainers are not solely presenters, there is an element of presentation in what we do. Therefore, it is important to master presentation skills.

Mel Silberman, colleague, author, consultant, and presenter extraordinaire, is an expert on active learning. Keep this concept in mind as you work through this step. It is easy for your participants to learn if the content is interesting and your presentation is smooth. It is even easier for them to learn if your presentation is action oriented.

Delivering a smooth presentation can mean many things and entire books—many of them—have been written about the topic of presentation skills. For our purpose, however, we will address just three areas I believe make the biggest difference. The areas are attending to what participants hear and see, staying organized while you are "on," and managing question-and-answer sessions—

STEP **7**

something many people get nervous about but shouldn't cause alarm if they have prepared.

This Step Is Important for Success

Although we trainers may not believe speaking skill is one of our strengths, there is an element of showmanship in what we do. We want to grab our participants' attention right from the start, we want participants to have fun, we want to present effectively so that participants leave with the skills and knowledge they came for, and we want to end with a closing that leaves participants anxious to reward the session with high marks on our smiley sheets. Yes, there is a bit of showmanship in all trainers. In fact, I have a friend who calls it "entertrainment."

If you've followed the training cycle or ADDIE, you have completed an assessment that confirms that training is necessary. Someone has invested time and energy in the design and development of a session that is packed with information, excellent participant materials, and a high-impact PowerPoint presentation. Your facilitation of the material and your presentation skills should match the quality of what has been invested so far.

Poor presentation techniques can get in the way of learning, so delivering a smooth presentation supports successful training.

POINTER

Don't force humor. Don't try to tell jokes if you are not a joke teller. Entertain within your comfort zone.

Delivery: Pay Attention to What They Hear and What They See

There's a great quote I heard once about presenters: "A good speech is less about what they say, and all about what we hear and what we see." It's true. Someone could be delivering fascinating information, but if the presenter is using a monotone, includes lots of fillers (um, ah, you know), and repeats irritating nervous gestures, it is almost impossible to continue to listen to the content.

Over the years I have found the preceding quote to be very true for anyone who is communicating. It may not be fair, but that is the way life is. So let's dig deeper into this "what we hear and what we see."

What Do Your Participants Hear?

The first half of your presentation's effectiveness deals with what people hear. You want the vocal part of your delivery to add vitality and energy to your ideas and concepts. Six characteristics make up the audio part of your presentation: projection, pitch, pace, pauses, enunciation, and fillers.

Projection is the loudness of the communication. Do you project loudly enough? How's your volume? Loudness is measured when air is expelled from the lungs. You expel the air with maximum force and intensity when you are yelling, and you use little force when you speak softly. The appropriateness of a loud or soft voice depends on the room size, how large your group is, and your need for vocal variety. Variations in volume can be used to indicate urgency, excitement, and importance in your presentation. If your participants can't hear your words, they can't learn.

Pitch refers to the variation of high and low tones in your voice. In a conversation pitch flows up and down the scale naturally. However, sometimes when trainers are in front of a group, their voices become dull and flat. They have narrowed the range of their pitch. To visualize pitch, think of two states: Kansas and Colorado. Kansas is flat. Say the state's name, "Kansas." It comes out flat with little variation in pitch. Now picture the

POINTER

Speak to the person who is the greatest distance from you. Your voice will naturally project farther.

STEP 7

state of Colorado with its rolling hills, mountains, valleys, streams, and lots of variety. Even when you say, "Colorado," your voice naturally rolls up and down the scale. Pitch variety adds interest to your voice. Even more important, it also helps you to emphasize significant ideas or to signal transitions. Both of these are important to keep your learners interested in what you are saying and to continue to stay on track with you as you change topics or add points.

Pace is the rate of delivery. Pace is determined by the duration of sound and the number of pauses between these sounds. You may speak words quickly or slowly. They may be clipped or drawn out. As with volume and pitch, the pace of your presentation can also signal importance. I like to use this example when I teach speaking skills. Say "$50,000" quickly, as if it is just a small amount of money. Now, say it again, this time slowing your pace and adding emphasis on every other syllable. Does the first amount sound small and trivial? Does the second amount sound more impressive, even though it is the same amount of money?

One of the things speech teachers like to recommend to students in college and high school courses is to change their pace. They find most presenters speak either too fast or too slow. I disagree. Instead, I believe the most important thing you can do for yourself as a presenter is to stay with a pace that is comfortable to you. Don't try to speed up or slow down. Why? Your brain is accustomed to working with your mouth in a certain cadence. When you change that rhythm, you often forget what you were going to say. Here are some ideas instead. If you are told you speak too rapidly, try punctuating your presentation with more pauses. That's right. Just close your mouth when you feel the next bucket of words start to tumble out. If, however, you are told you speak too slowly, evaluate yourself on three things. First, make sure you are using no fillers. Fillers are much more noticeable if you speak slowly. Second, be certain you are moving directly through your information and that you are not repeating the same information. And third, know your material cold. Practice your content aloud several extra times.

Pauses can add emphasis more than anything we have mentioned so far. A judiciously placed pause, before or after an idea, can focus attention right where you want it and can leave your participants hanging onto the most critical idea you have to present. Pauses help your focus, too. They allow you time to think. Pauses also give you time to observe the participants for feedback. Pauses are the sign of a seasoned presenter because most inexperienced presenters are uncomfortable with silence. Practice your pauses.

Enunciation is critical for your participants to understand and learn easily. Speaking articulately and pronouncing your words clearly and distinctly is a sign of a pro. Learn to enunciate clearly. Be careful that you do not run your words together. And finally, don't swallow the ends of your sentences. When your words trail off, your learners will have difficulty hearing the complete message. Speak strongly, enunciating clearly through the end of every sentence.

Fillers are those nasty little nonsounds that sneak in when we aren't listening to ourselves. Um, ah, and ah, er, okay, ya know, like. All are examples of fillers. They can hypnotize your participants into a trance or can grate on their innermost nerves. Have you ever counted the "ya knows" used by your least favorite college professor? Whether your participants are counting your "okays" or not, you can be certain that they will not hear your content if the fillers are distracting. The sad thing is that most of us do not hear our own fillers.

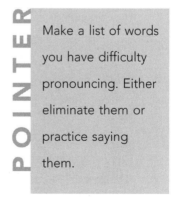

POINTER

Make a list of words you have difficulty pronouncing. Either eliminate them or practice saying them.

There is one surefire way to eliminate your fillers. You will need to hire yourself an Um Counter, someone who will listen to your presentation and provide you with feedback about how many fillers you use per minute and which ones you use. Another possibility is to record your presentation and listen to it after the training session. I used this technique to help reduce my use of fillers. When I did this, the shock seemed to awaken something so that I could finally hear my fillers. If you are struggling with fillers, cleaning them up won't happen overnight. If you do not currently hear your own fillers, it may take some time before you do. Just keep working at listening to yourself.

What Do Your Participants See?

The other half of your presentation technique is what your learners see. They should see a trainer who is confident, competent, and organized and who is ready to convey an interesting and exciting message.

Body stance is one of the first things participants notice. Good posture and poise convey confidence in your message, making your participants interested in learning more. When you first arrive at the front of the room, plant your feet about as wide as your shoulders or an inch or two wider. This helps to prevent you from shifting your weight. Moving around and among the participants is good. It uses up some of your nervous energy and helps to create a natural and comfortable environment. However, repetitive moves, such as pacing back and forth in the same spot, shuffling your feet, or crossing your legs can be distracting and draw attention away from your face.

Try to always face your participants. Learn to talk and walk backwards so you rarely need to break eye contact with your participants. How about sitting? Sitting changes the tone of your presentation, which is good when you do it purposefully. The operative word is "purposefully." It would be rare, but I think you may sit or even lean against a table. Your stance then says, "This is informal." The tenor of the presentation has changed. I have on occasion purposefully pulled a chair to the middle of the room, and while sitting had a heart-to-heart discussion with a group that was disagreeable. So the question is, what is your purpose for sitting? What atmosphere do you want to convey?

Gestures frequently present a dilemma to presenters. Your hands seem to work perfectly well until you stand in front of a group of people and then they just seem to be in the way! Gestures are important to convey your enthusiasm and to help your participants follow your presentation. Keep them natural. If you start with your hands at your sides, they will start working naturally. Think about speaking and gesturing to those seated farthest from you. This enhances your gestures, as well as your projection. Avoid crossing your arms, playing with your marker, rolling your notes, or touching your head. Use gestures that are natural to you, and add those that help to convey your message.

How about putting your hands in your pockets? This question is similar to the one about sitting. It depends. Are you putting your hands in your pockets because you are nervous or they feel awkward and you don't know what to do with them? Or are you putting your hands in your pockets because you are relaxed and you want to send a message of relaxation to your audience. If you are putting your hands in your pockets for the first reason, then the answer is no. Don't do it. You will just get into trouble jangling change. However, if your reason is to send a message of relaxation, then fine, go ahead. (And remember to empty your pockets before your session.)

Facial expression should be congruent with your words. In fact, your face can express more than your words! Facial change is a good indication of a relaxed

POINTER

If you want to keep your hands out of your pockets put something that you don't usually find in your pocket, such as a wadded up piece of paper, to remind you to remove them.

STEP 7

speaker. Use it to add emphasis to your message and to display energy. Be aware of your expressions and what they may convey. You of course also need to be aware of the times when you should not display expression. For example, those times when you need to maintain your cool when dealing with a disruptive participant.

Early in my career, I was surprised when a participant said to me, "You don't want us to ask questions." This was of course exactly the opposite of what I wanted. I did want them to ask all the questions necessary to understand the skills they were learning. When I asked why she made the statement she said, "Whenever we ask questions you frown." Wow! I was unaware of frowning. I finally realized that when I was asked questions, I would concentrate on what they were saying. When I concentrate my face appears to be frowning. It was a great lesson. What are your facial expressions saying about you?

Eye contact is important in all conversations, but particularly so for trainers. In the United States, eye contact represents caring and understanding and builds trust. Good eye contact builds rapport with your participants. Avoid looking at the ceiling. And don't just sweep the participants or try to get by with looking at the tops of their heads. People know if you are making eye contact or not. Good eye contact is a tool. It lets you see participants' facial expressions, allowing you to know if they understand what is happening or if they agree with you.

I find that most trainers ignore the 25 percent of the participants who are seated closest to the front on the trainer's dominant side. Are you aware of where your eyes are focused and at whom you are looking? Be sure to look at all of your participants. By the way, I have noticed that good eye contact decreases the number of fillers a presenter uses. Somehow we can't look someone in the eye and say, "um!" as easily as when we are looking at our notes or the back of the room.

Eye contact is a cultural preference. It is not viewed the same everywhere. If you are training in another country or training other cultures in the United States, you will of course need to respect other values. Some cultures consider it rude or aggressive. Be familiar with the culture of your participants.

Nervousness is displayed in numerous ways: pacing or swaying, fidgeting with a pen, jingling change in your pocket, perspiring, shaking, clearing your throat, grimacing, appearing tense, and dozens of other things. However, if you have interesting content, your participants will never notice that you are nervous.

The number one rule regarding nervousness is, "Do not tell your participants that you are nervous." If you don't tell them, chances are your participants will never know! Here are some tips to address your nervousness:

- First recognize that you will be nervous. Know what your signs of nervousness are and then say to yourself, "Oh there it is—that butterfly in my stomach. That's my nervous signal." Then move on.
- Find the best way to relax before beginning. This might be a couple of head and shoulder rolls; it might be a couple of isometric exercises or deep breathing. Do what works best for you.
- Arrive early to take ownership of the training room. When your "guests" arrive it will be as if you are on your home field.
- Wear clothes that you feel great in. It is best to avoid a new suit, new shoes, or a new haircut.
- Organize yourself. In fact, supersize your organization. Knowing that everything is where it belongs and is ready to go will relax you.
- Got a security blanket? Use it. Mine is to always have a glass of

POINTER

On the first day, while the host is introducing me, I like to take two or three very deep breaths. No one sees it. I am getting oxygen to my brain and centering myself.

STEP **7**

water and a stack of paper towels on the table with my supplies—you never know. Besides the water is handy for a dry throat or when I need a pause to remember what I was saying!

◆ Tell yourself that your participants want you to succeed. Send yourself positive messages, "I've got this covered! It's going to be grrreeaaat!"

◆ Get participants involved early. You could ask a question, start a discussion, or organize an activity. After that it will feel more like a two-way conversation.

Remember that even if you are nervous, your participants will rarely notice it unless you tell them and then they will start looking for the signs. They may be thinking about how lucky they are that it is you in front of the room instead of them! It may be somewhat comforting to know that even the most experienced trainers, actors, actresses, politicians, and stars experience nervousness before speaking to a large group of people.

If you focus on your participants and their needs, you take attention off yourself and get over the butterflies fluttering in your stomach sooner. To get those butterflies to fly in formation you must first remember that nervousness is natural. Try the techniques in Table 7.1 to address specific nervous symptoms.

Plan for what you will drink.

◆ Avoid coffee. If you are new to training, your nervousness may prevent you from counting how many cups you are drinking. Adding additional caffeine to your presentation anxiety may create a bodacious buzz!

◆ Avoid dairy products, for example, milk or yogurt, to prevent mucus build-up, requiring you to clear your throat.

- Avoid sugary liquids such as fruit juices and soda, they coat your vocal cords.
- Avoid icy beverages because they constrict your vocal cords.
- Okay! What's left? Room temperature or cool water, warm water with lemon, herbal teas, decaffeinated teas or coffee. This is just to get you through the first couple of hours. Later when your nerves have calmed down you can switch to one of your favorite drinks (nonalcoholic, of course!)

Stay Organized

Organization redeems all trainers. If you are organized lots of other things will be easier. Listed here are three items you should consider to keep yourself organized: A working agenda or design matrix, ways to stay organized during the session, and thoughts about the use of notes (to keep your brain organized!)

Session Agenda

Your company most likely has some form of session agenda or design matrix for the training that you deliver. I use a design matrix like the example found in Table 7.2. I print it on brightly colored paper, like lemon yellow, and then add my own comments. The reason I use a lemon-yellow paper is so that at any time I can look at the mess on the table and find the lemon yellow peeking out from under everything else. This matrix is critical because it is the key to keeping me on schedule.

What do I add to the matrix? I write the actual times, such as 9:40 or 2:15, so that I can easily glance at the time an activity is supposed to begin and compare it with my watch. I'll know in an instant whether I am ahead, behind, or on schedule. I highlight unique areas, for example, if I need to solicit a participant to do something during the break. I use a colored marker to note special equipment or activities, and I underline places where I need to

TABLE 7.1
Ideas for Specific Nervous Symptoms

Nervousness is nothing more than a fear reflex. It is natural and occurs because your body is getting ready for fight or flight. These ideas do not remove the nervousness. They may mask it or provide you with a temporary crutch.

Shakiness	Stand near a table and use it as a touchstone; avoid caffeine.
Moving or swaying	Plant your feet a full shoulder's width apart.
Trembling legs	Don't try to control them; isolate one muscle group and shake it out before you begin.
Sweaty palms	Try talc or antiperspirant (experiment with it first).
Squeaky voice	No iced beverages; try lemon and honey in warm decaffeinated tea. Try "Throat Coat," a commercial tea.
Throat mucus	Drink warm tea with lemon; avoid dairy products.
Dry throat	Bite on a lemon or use mouth spray; have water available.
Fillers	Write a large "UM" on your notes to remind you; maintain good eye contact.
Facial expressions	Greet people early and think of them as your friends when you see them in the audience.
Jangle change	Empty your pockets.
Flushed skin	Wear red or darker colors to camouflage it.
Fast pulse rate	Breathe deeply.
Twitching	Experiment between training sessions; try rubbing, tapping, or gently pinching yourself.
Rapid speech	Write a cue to "slow down" on your notes; practice pausing.

give the participants handouts. Also, when I need to put items on the participants' tables during the breaks, I will note that also. At other times a special setup may be required to prepare for the next day. I will make that note at the end of the day's agenda. At the top of the page I may also note the name of the facilities and/or

TABLE 7.2

Design Matrix Example

Phase 1: Contact and Agreement Time: 125 Minutes

Objectives:

◆ State how to build a relationship with the client.
◆ Identify whether a client is ready.
◆ Develop effective questions.
◆ Reach agreement on expectations.

Time	Topic/ Content	Learning Method	Materials/ Media	Length	Pages
	Introduction to Module	Lecturette	Wall chart	5 min	1–3
	Credibility and You	Small- or large-group discussion		15 min	4–6
	Building Client Relationships	Practice with a simple model	Flipchart	30 min	7
	Establish Effective Questions	Small-group activity based on Case Study: Part 1: list questions	Case study input; Client Readiness Checklist	35 min	8–9
	Reach Agreement on Expectations	Use the questions created in previous activity to reach agreement (pairs with observer)	Project Acceptance Agreement; Contracting Checklist	30 min	10
	Reflections on the Future	Personal review and planning	Personal Mastery Plan	10 min	11

STEP 7

IT coordinators and their phone numbers in case I have an emergency.

I find the matrix to be one of the best tools for keeping me organized and keeping the training session on time.

Ways to Stay Organized

A training session has a lot of moving parts. Staying organized and maintaining your sanity may require a few tips to help you. Here are a few lessons I've learned over the years:

◆ Straighten up your presentation table during breaks. You can put your notes back in the three-ring notebook while participants are asking you their questions or sharing their deepest darkest secrets (usually about their bosses).

◆ Have a plan for your presentation table that you use over and over. Index cards placed here, extra pencil here, trainer's manual there, and water in this spot. Sounds trivial, but when you are trying to juggle three things at once and you know exactly where your masking tape is located, you will thank yourself.

◆ Lay out all the handouts required in the order in which they will be used. If the session is a multiday session, place a colored piece of paper (different color from the matrix discussed previously so you don't get confused) between the handouts from one day to the next. If there are lots of handouts, have a second table to the side where the handouts for the next day are kept.

◆ Count out the handouts for each table and crisscross them for ease of passing them out. This is totally dependent upon the amount of time I have between activities.

◆ If certificates are involved, always double check the spelling as soon as possible, which unfortunately may not be until the day the session starts with no way to correct them on site. Call the organization or department required to complete the certificates and have them verify that a corrected certificate will be sent to the participant. I still hand the certificate to the participant at the end of the training session even if there is a spelling error. And I apologize and let the participant know the plan for replacing it with a corrected one. Most people understand and appreciate that this personal detail was addressed.

◆ Wear a jacket with a pocket. This is where you can keep the remote for the PowerPoint presentation. Nothing is more annoying than losing the remote and being tied to the projector when you really ought to be circulating among the participants.

◆ Always request that the projector be placed on the front table instead of the projection cart that IT likes to deliver it on. Placing it on the table eliminates the cart and the need to walk around it. Condensing all the equipment, materials, supplies, and notes to one table gives a sense of order—kind of like circling the wagons and having everything safely in one central place!

◆ Trainers' manuals sold by training suppliers have not usually been written for a real trainer. I am not sure who they are for, but I rarely find one that meets my needs. I suggest that as one of your methods for preparing for the session, you create your own set of notes for the training session.

Thoughts on Notes

I am frequently asked about using notes. Should they be used? Should they be on note cards? Should they be in outline format? Should they contain the entire script? I generally say yes. I don't mean to sound flippant, but notes are a personal thing. You need to create notes that work for you. The serious part is the "yes." Use notes—but don't be dependent on them. You will feel more comfortable and your participants will appreciate that you do not lose your place. Notes are important to keep you organized, helping you to be successful with this step.

Notes are important to this step to success. Whether you are facilitating a three-hour or a three-day training session, no one expects you to remember everything you need to say. And your participants don't want to hear a canned speech either. You need to train from the same notes that you practiced with. Your notes should become an extension of yourself so that you require just a glance toward your notes to remind you of what you need to do or say next. Your participants want you to interact with them, not your notes.

You have at least three choices for formatting your notes. You can use the facilitator's guide that came with the training program. It usually has everything you need. The drawback is that it may have more than you need with little room for personalization. You could also start with a clean sheet of paper and create an entire set of your own notes. They will be completely personalized, but this will take a long time. The third choice is to begin with the same pages the participants will use and add your notes to them.

I prefer to use the same notebook or handouts that the participants have in front of them. I add notes about the content in bullet format. I generally list just a couple of words that will jog my memory. For example, instead of writing out the entire story I use as an example of how the gift of creativity can be taken away at an early age, I will write, "Thad kindergarten," which is enough to remind me of the three-minute story. I also add brief notes about activities, how I'll put participants into small groups, and so on. This becomes my personalized facilitator's guide.

I also like to train from the same pages that the participants are using because it is easy for me to glance at my notes and say, "You should be on page 48," or "Turn back to the earlier chapter on page 13." I find this an easy way to keep on track without any hassle at all. I sometimes observe trainers struggling to train from poorly designed facilitator's guides provided for the session. If it works for you, do it. I find using the facilitator's guide as a "guide" (just as it is called) to suggest what I might do or say a good start. From then on I personalize it for the participants, using their examples and their department's or industry's jargon. This activity helps me prepare for the session. It gives me a sense of ownership of the content.

How can you use notes effectively? Here are some thoughts:

◆ Notes should be considered a guide to keep you on track and on time.

◆ Practice with your notes. They should become a support system that you know well and can rely on.

◆ Learn to hold your notes comfortably and unobtrusively. You'll need to tape yourself or present in front of a full-length mirror to decide what works for you and how you look best. I usually just keep three or four pages in my hand and take a peek whenever I need to.

◆ Don't fold or staple your notes. Folding weakens the paper and makes the pages want to flop over as you are holding them. A staple prevents flexibility. In addition, you'll appear more professional if you do not need to flip the page over as if you are holding some long "bill of lading."

◆ Be sure the pages are clearly numbered. If you use my system, you may at times add other pages among the participant's pages. If you do so, mark clearly where the page belongs, for example, 4.5 belongs between pages 4 and 5. This makes it easy to place the notes in correct order when you are putting them away.

◆ Use ways to cue yourself about where to look for specific information in your notes. Highlight, underlining, using a different color of marker or font—all are possibilities.

Notes are an important part of ensuring that you deliver a smooth presentation. Try out different formats and observe what other trainers do with their notes.

STEP 7

POINTER

Become intimate with your notes. Deliver from the same notes with which you practiced.

Managing Participants' Questions

Many trainers begin their sessions by saying, "Stop me at any time to ask questions." That's a good start. What's more important is how they respond to participants' questions. Even if you do want participants to ask questions throughout your presentation, you still want to qualify your comment by addressing those times when participants ask questions a bit too early. Decide how you'll handle that.

If you get a difficult question you may wish to turn it back to the group. Remember, "I don't know, but I will find out and let you know by_____," is an acceptable response. Never try to bluff your way through an answer.

You may need to paraphrase the question to ensure that you understand the question and that everyone else has heard it. This paraphrase also buys you a bit of time to think about your response.

If you get a question that is too far outside the content area or narrowly focused to the individual's needs, you may wish to volunteer to speak with the individual at the break or after your session.

STEP 7

POINTER

If you need additional thinking time, take a sip of the water on your table. It clears your throat and clears your mind.

The use of a parking lot is also helpful for questions that are just a bit outside the topic area if you think others might benefit from the answer, but the timing is not right. Encourage people to use the parking lot by modeling what to do; ask the responder of the first out-of-context question to write it on a sticky note and place it on the parking lot.

You may also receive questions that may be negatively motivated, questions that are meant to delay a difficult task (such as in a speaking-skills session), questions asked to impress others, questions meant to trip up the trainer, or questions meant to highlight a negative situation. How you handle these will vary in every instance, but here are some guidelines:

- Repeat the question to give you some time to think about your response.
- Paraphrase the question to give it a more positive spin.
- Keep your response short and on target.
- End your response while looking at someone else so that the questioner is not encouraged to follow with another question.
- If the question is completely off track and inappropriate you might say something like, "Let's discuss that off line."

When you respond, make good eye contact, but not just with the person who asked the question. Continue to include the entire group in your response. If you don't, others begin to feel left out; sometimes making eye contact with only one person encourages another question and before you know it you have a two-way conversation occurring with the rest of the room completely outside the training discussion.

Observe the questioner's body language. If you are not sure that your response was focused correctly, follow up with, "Is that what you were looking for?" or "Is that what you needed to know?"

If you want to encourage questions, think about how you want to phrase your request. "What questions do you have?" is more encouraging than the close-ended question, "Do you have any questions?" Minor difference in words, but it may make a big difference to some of your participants.

POINTER

Keep a list of the tips you most want to remember in your trainer's guide.

TABLE 7.3
Guidelines for Answering Questions

- Anticipate your participants' questions.
- Inform participants of your expectations for questions early in the session.
- Listen carefully to each question for both content (what is asked) and intent (what is meant).
- Paraphrase the question to ensure that everyone heard it.
- Ask for clarification if necessary.
- Keep your answer short and on target.
- Direct your response to the entire group, not just the person who asked the question.
- Verify your response with, "Is that what you were looking for?" if necessary.
- Avoid showing your feelings to a hostile questioner.
- If you don't know an answer, redirect it to the audience, to another source, or state your follow-up plan for getting the information.
- "I don't know" is an acceptable answer.
- If a topic is extremely emotional empathize with the feelings of your audience.
- Maintain both verbal and nonverbal control.
- Restate the question when
    - Question needs clarification.
    - You have a large group.
    - The question is "loaded" and needs to be reworded.
    - You need thinking time.

Review Table 7.3, Guidelines for Answering Questions, as a reminder of some of the things you can do to enhance your ability to smoothly respond to questions. You may wish to copy this page to help keep good question management in mind before your next training session.

Asking Questions

As a trainer, you will also ask questions. Use a variety of questioning techniques to encourage participation: open, closed, or leading. Think about the purpose of the question:

- Are you looking for a correct answer?
- Are you trying to create a discussion?
- Are you trying to stimulate thinking?
- Are you trying to tap a known expert in the group?
- Are you trying to increase participation from a specific individual?
- Are you trying to balance participation?
- Are you trying to clarify a comment or question?
- Are you trying to get the group back on track?
- Are you asking them to take the information to the next step to apply it outside the classroom?

You need to determine the purpose of the question to ensure that you will get the response you want.

I don't believe in catching people off guard—like your fourth-grade teacher did when you were gazing out the window. We all take mini vacations. To avoid embarrassing your participants, state their names first and then ask the question.

Pause after asking a question. Trainers can be uncomfortable with silence, so if no one answers within a few seconds they repeat the question again and then finally answer it themselves. The message you send when you do this is, "If we wait long enough, the trainer will answer the question."

Whether you are asking or answering questions, learn to listen carefully. Listen for both the content and the intent of

STEP 7

the statement or question. You will want to understand the speaker's perspective.

Delivering a smooth presentation is an important part of every trainer's job. You can do it if you attend to what participants hear and see, stay organized, and learn to manage participants' questions.

Personal Steps to Success

1. Ask a colleague to sit in and provide you with feedback on your training style. This will be most helpful if you provide a list of specific things you want the individual to look for, such as any fillers you use or how well you make eye contact.
2. Join Toastmasters or take a speaking class at your local community college to get more feedback about your speaking, presentation, and training style.
3. Make a list of your nervous symptoms and identify what you might do differently to reduce or mask the symptoms. Use some of the ideas in Table 7.1. Use your ideas as you prepare and practice for your next training session.
4. Put a plan together for how you will stay organized during your next training session.
5. Anticipate six questions your participants will have during your next training session. Identify how you will respond.

Make It Interesting—Use Lively Openings, Transitions, and Powerful Closings

Developing lively openings

Planning for functional transitions

Ending with powerful closings

Too often all of our time is spent on the content of a training design and its delivery. To ensure successful training you need to allocate your time to accommodate three other areas of the training program: the opening, transitions, and the closing.

The opening must be lively and grab attention early. It sets the stage for all that follows. Transitions must be invisible but serve participants well, helping them move from one place to another. The ending, similarly, plays the important role of bringing closure and leaving participants with an understanding of what they need to do next.

STEP 8

This Step Is Important for Success

Trainers have so many things to do and think about, they may not have time to even consider how important it is to grab participants' attention right from the start. They may have never thought about the role that transitions play in helping participants grasp concepts and relate them to other concepts. They may not have realized that without planning, their training may end with a thud, instead of a bang.

This step is important for success because it ensures that learners' needs are met from beginning to end. It expects trainers to get off on the right foot, bring closure appropriately, and assist participants in making necessary transitions easily throughout the rest of the session.

Enhancing content with a lively opening, functional transitions, and a powerful closing is an often overlooked step to successful training.

Lively Openings

First impressions are critical to your success. The opening of your training session may very well be the most important part of the entire training. The first 30 minutes sets the stage for what is to come. It informs your participants about the content, the tone, the goals, and the trainer's nature. If you refer back to Step 3 you can easily incorporate Malcolm Knowles's six assumptions into an effective opening. Your opening should be:

- ◆ **Informative as well as creative.** You'll want to inform your participants about the course objectives and what they can expect to learn. This is a chance for you to demonstrate that the session will be action oriented and participative. Your opening should show participants that you will rely on their input and that they have the ability to direct their own learning experience. You can model and set the stage during your opening.
- ◆ **Practical and also promote excitement**. Participants bring a wealth of experience to the session. They will be interested to learn how that experience will be incorporated into this new material and what they can learn from

TABLE 8.1
Open Your Training Session with PUNCH

Promote interest and enthusiasm

Understand participants' needs

Note the ground rules and administrative needs

Clarify expectations

Help everyone get to know each other

others in the session. Participants like to know who else is in the training session, how the training session will help them in their daily life or work, and how it might solve problems they are currently experiencing.

◆ **Helpful as well as enthusiastic.** It is helpful to participants to know how the session will unfold, when lunch and breaks will occur, and for other logistical questions to be addressed. When you do this quickly and with enthusiasm they can set these concerns aside and focus on the learning before them.

ASTD's Training Certificate course offers guidance on how to open your training session with PUNCH. The mnemonic covers all the aspects that you should consider for the opening of training (see Table 8.1).

The first thing you should do is to start on time. Starting late sets a precedent that will only create problems during the rest of

STEP **8**

the session. Let's consider some of the things you can do in each of these five PUNCH steps to facilitate a lively opening.

Promote Interest and Enthusiasm

Engage your participants right from the start. Don't begin your session with mind-numbing sign-in forms or dull administrative tasks such as how to get your parking ticket validated. Yes, these are important and should be addressed during the opening, but do it as you transition to the first content module—after you start your session with PUNCH and before the first break.

It's wise to invest time in perfecting your opening. Rehearse the first hour several extra times. Starting off positively and gaining your participants' confidence will pay off well for the rest of the session. You know what they say about a first impression . . .

I love to use props. Props can be used as metaphors for the training session. As soon as you pull out a stack of t-shirts or building tools or a crystal ball you'll have participants' attention and interest. Don't do it just for the theatrics, however. Use props because they will help participants remember key information or to lead you into an activity.

POINTER

Memorize the first few sentences you will deliver during your opening. This is a real stress reducer.

T-shirts? How can you use t-shirts? I sometimes use t-shirts when I facilitate a team-building session. I begin by saying, "Some people say that you can't tell a book by its cover. I believe, however, that you can tell a person by the t-shirt he or she wears." I then hold up a couple of t-shirts that tell something about me: my ASTD t-shirt, which tells about my professional affiliation; a Green Bay Packers t-shirt; and one that says, "A woman's place is in the house ... and in the senate" or another one to get a laugh. I give participants a colorful sheet of paper that has the outline of a t-shirt and ask them to draw a picture or write a motto that tells us something about them. I share one that I have prepared as a model.

They introduce themselves using the t-shirt and tape it to the wall. These t-shirts are used throughout the team-building session. To build the team, I ask participants to write on others' t-shirts things such as, "I like the way you ... " or "I am pleased you are on our team so that we can ...." I use them in other ways, too. For example, I use different colors of paper and use the colors to form at least one small group during the session.

Again, don't use props just for the theatrics. My objectives for using them with team-building sessions are to

◆ get participant's attention immediately
◆ set the stage that this session will be active
◆ help participants learn something about each other they may not have known before
◆ create a theme that can be used throughout the session to reinforce other concepts and to build the team.

Your opening, and in particular your icebreaker, is a great time to promote interest and enthusiasm.

Understand Participants' Needs

Someone somewhere along the process has conducted an official needs assessment that resulted in this training session. However, it is always good to conduct a mini needs assessment up front. A simple show of hands with several well-selected questions will help you understand participants' knowledge, skills, experiences, and expertise. This gives you an immediate understanding of the level of experience you have in the room.

There are other ways to identify participants' needs. You can ask them about their hopes and fears or the greatest problem they hope this training session will solve. I also like to conduct a self-assessment early in the session. Participants get to read the topics we will cover via the assessment. Then I ask which areas they have rated lowest and highest. This information gives me an idea of the group's greatest needs.

When you understand your participants' needs you have the ability to tailor the content and the amount of time spent on the content to the requirements of your group.

Note the Ground Rules and Administrative Needs

In Steps 1 and 5 we mentioned Maslow's Hierarchy of Needs. This is one place where they are significant. You are wise if you address your participants' physiological and safety needs up front so they can climb up the hierarchy faster.

Certainly one of the standard ways to do that is to create a list of ground rules. Because some ground rules are given, it will save you time if you post those first and ask participants to add others that they desire. Post the ground rules for easy reference throughout the training session. I find myself referring to them on occasion if a question arises (what's said in the session stays in the session) or for disruptive participants (no sidebar discussion). Be sure to use the ground rules as a tool to manage the session for all participants.

Attend to any administrative needs briefly. Post the list on a flipchart page so that you can move through it quickly. I generally make these announcements after the icebreaker, which I know is different from what you experience in most training sessions. In fact announcements are treated as a "by the way" after all of the other more exciting aspects of an opening with PUNCH are taken care of.

Clarify Expectations

Participants want to know what they will learn and why. Clarify both your expectations as well as theirs. A good activity to use to accomplish this is to ask them what they hope to learn from the session. Confirm their ideas and be ready to tell them if something is not going to be covered.

Review the agenda's main points and the objectives for the session. The main reason for the cursory review is not to state everything that is written on the agenda, but instead to show the flow and the movement of the content and how the agenda supports the objectives.

Clarifying expectations prevents misunderstandings later about what the participants thought the session would cover.

Help Everyone Get to Know Each Other

Because participants learn as much (or more) from each other as they do from the material, ensure that they know each other right from the start. Certainly you can go around the room using the old tried-and-true four introductory questions:

- ◆ Your name?
- ◆ Where you work?
- ◆ Your expectations?
- ◆ Something interesting about you?

POINTER

Post phone numbers you have to share with participants on a flipchart page. If you don't you will find yourself repeating them several times.

POINTER

If a request cannot be met during the session, inform the group how they can obtain the requested content, recommend a book, or follow up after the session.

STEP **8**

But there are more interesting ways to make this happen. For example, identify one early issue about the topic, have participants form small groups (I prefer them to leave their seats and meet in designated places in the room), have them introduce themselves to the small group, and then have them wrestle with the issue their group has been assigned.

Get all participants involved early. If you intend to have a highly participative session (and you should), find ways to initiate participation within the first five minutes. A simple show of hands (such as during your mini needs assessment) is one way to get started. A better way is to get them out of their seats, meeting other participants while involved in an icebreaker.

Did you know that an icebreaker in the shipping world is a vessel designed to clear an opening in frozen water that allows for the flow of other ships? This is a good metaphor for what you are trying to accomplish with an icebreaker in your training sessions. You are trying to clear an opening in a cool atmosphere that allows communication and relationship building to "flow."

Trainers sometimes select icebreakers out of a book of 1,001 icebreakers. That's one way to do it. A better way is to customize the icebreaker. You may find something that is close to your purpose and tailor it to meet your needs. Like anything in your training session, the icebreaker should have a solid purpose. I believe that every icebreaker should:

◆ **Relate to the content.** Everyone is very busy today. Chances are the organization has asked you to squeeze more into your training day than you would like. So make the icebreaker work for you. Use it to get discussion started about the topic. Use it to uncover participants' expectations. This will also ensure a natural flow from the opening into the content of the training session.

◆ **Set the tone of the session.** Icebreakers can be fun, but if you are addressing a serious topic it may be difficult to make the transition. The tone may also refer to how you anticiate the learning to occur. This is an opportunity to encourage sharing, working in teams, speaking out, laughing, empathizing, disagreeing, using processes, or a host of other aspects that define the tone.

♦ **Demonstrate the level of involvement participants can expect.** If you anticipate that participants will interact with each other and this will be how much of the learning will occur, use the icebreaker to establish this expectation. Allow the icebreaker to model how learning will occur.

♦ **Form groups that will best integrate individuals into the larger group.** An icebreaker can encourage participants to meet as many others as possible and get a tidbit of information from each. It can also require a few people in a small group to gather a bit more information about the people in their group. And in another model an icebreaker can pair people up to learn more in-depth information so that they could introduce each other.

♦ **Afford you an opportunity to observe the group and learn more about them.** Circulate during the icebreaker, observing individuals and teams. Who seems to be taking the lead? Who is organizing? Who is holding back? Who is competitive? Who is dominating? This will give you information about the best way to work with individuals and how to form small groups in the future.

POINTER

The tried-and-true bingo icebreaker is the best example of how to encourage participants to meet as many others as possible. The bingo card comprises a five by five matrix, 25 squares with a different descriptor in each square, such as "drives a red car." Participants meet by having other participants sign a square that describes him or her.

STEP **8**

Icebreaker Process

To encompass all of the preceding suggestions I have an icebreaker process that I have incorporated into a couple of newly developed training sessions. I work in themes that may make this easier, although you certainly do not need to do so. Working with the topics, I select four to six issues, concerns, ideas, or relationships related to the topic. The goal is to get participants talking about the topic within the first 10 minutes of starting the workshop. These categories should be more opinion based than knowledge based.

Here are the basic directions:

- A symbol or object representing each of the four to six issues, topics, concerns, or relationships is posted or placed in the room. Locations are far enough away from each other so that small groups can form and communicate without disturbing the others. My preference is to use the four corners of the room and add other spaces if needed.

- Participants select one of the issues, topics, relationships, or other categories based on my description. I may also have the descriptions posted on a flipchart or on a PowerPoint slide.

- Further directions are given to prevent too many people from joining one group. If I want every issue discussed, I take time before the session to figure out the maximum number of people who can be at each spot. For example, if I have five categories and 23 people, I might say, "Have a first and second choice in mind. Go to your first choice unless there are already five people there, then move to your second choice." In the example, every category would be covered, at the maximum, four categories will have five people and the fifth will have three. Having an equal number of people does not matter, but each category must be represented.

- Once participants have arrived at their category, I provide directions that include
  - introduce yourselves
  - state the department or organization where you work
  - describe the assignment.

Let me share the generic objectives of these icebreakers and then I will give you a couple of examples. The objectives are to

- meet other participants
- save time with introductions
- get to the content immediately
- lead in to the first topic that will be discussed or provide an introduction to the overall topic
- give the trainer a chance to observe individuals in action.

Here are two examples that have worked well. The first involves building a leadership development program using the analogy that building such a program is like building a house. It requires different roles that are represented by items placed around the room. For example, it requires

- an architect, represented by a blueprint on the wall
- a general contractor, represented by a calculator
- a superintendent, represented by a yellow plastic hardhat
- a member of the trades, represented by a hammer
- a decorator, represented by scissors.

After a brief description of the roles, I ask each participant to select a role and go to the one that most represents the role they play in building their leadership development program. Once there, a PowerPoint slide asks them and their "building crew" to introduce themselves, why they selected that role, and to identify ways that building a leadership development program is like building a house.

A second example is for a facilitating change session and the theme is "the change journey." Street signs are posted in the four

STEP 8

corners of the room. I ask them to move to the corner that most closely matches their perception of change. Once they are in position, have them introduce themselves and discuss with fellow participants why they selected the sign they did.

I have them stay positioned under the chosen signs and ask each group's representative to report to the larger group. The signs are printed with these four "street crossings," and participants give responses similar to those listed beneath the sign.

- **Normal and Expected Street Sign**
    - People grow; organizations grow. We need to know that change will occur.
    - Change happens all the time.
- **New and Exciting Street Sign**
    - Fun, it means growth; if not, it is boring.
    - Change means synergy to keep things exciting.
- **Daunting but Necessary Street Sign**
    - Facilitating change is necessary.
    - New organizational development is necessary.
- **Difficult and Worthwhile Street Sign**
    - "Got to pay the dues if you are going to play the blues. . . . "
    - Change carries emotional attachment.
    - The organization will be healthier in the end.

I make some closing remarks and the session has started, bringing all the participants into the change discussion.

There are many more things that you can do to ensure that your training session will open with PUNCH. You may wish to use some of the books listed in the Resources for Trainers at the end of this volume.

Functional Transitions

Transitions are important to make certain that your participants follow you from one place to another. If you've ever been a participant yourself, you know how easy it is to drift off to take a mini vacation. The trainer makes a comment about the Blue Water Accrual System, and you are off thinking about the vacation that will take you next to **blue water** in Hawaii next month. All of a sudden you realize that you have been packing a suitcase and scuba diving instead of learning about the new accounting system you need to implement in your department. You look at the screen but it is blank and then the trainer says, "Now that we've finished part five dash c, let's turn the page and examine the top of the form, part five dash d." Thank heaven for good transitions!

This happens to all participants. As a trainer you want to remember that transitions are important and serve an important function for your learners. Not only do they help participants find their places after short mini vacations, they ensure a smooth presentation by leading participants from one general area to another.

A transition does the work of a map. It allows participants to see the big picture and, at the same time, see how things are connected. Here is a handful of ideas:

- Build in transitions when you are designing. If you can't immediately see the logical flow from one topic to another, you can't expect your participants to see it.
- Use themes. As mentioned earlier, themes keep me on track and provide a visual for participants to easily follow from one place to another. You can also identify themes that relate the previous content to the current content. For example, you might tell them how the information from the case study they just completed prepares them for the next section.
- Use the model. If you have developed a model for the program, post a large one on the wall. Just the act of showing the movement from one module to the next reminds

STEP 8

participants of the big picture and how the modules work together.

♦ Use the agenda. When you move from one topic area to another bring participants' attention back to the agenda.

♦ Use a building-block approach. Summarize the concepts from the current module and point out how they will be the foundation for the next module.

♦ Use verbal cues. Bring closure to the current module before you introduce the next one. For example, you could say, "Now that we have completed X, it is easy to see how Y must follow."

♦ Use participants. Invite participants to summarize what was just covered.

Trainers need to be aware of how they are transitioning participants to new material. Transitions needs some thought and planning. I like to mark my transitions in the margin of my notes. Transitions are not something that participants will usually notice. However, if your participants are lost, ask how well your transitions led them from one place to another. Perhaps your transitions were the culprit and could use some improvement.

Powerful Closings

Participants need a sense of closure at the end of a session. This is true for the end of each day as well as the end of the entire session. If you've ever seen an old Warner Bros. cartoon, you know that Porky Pig's signature line at the end, "Th-th-th-th-that's all folks," is not enough to close a training session. However, too often that's what it feels like when the design ran a little long because more content was squeezed into the time allotted than could be managed effectively. Things can become rushed at the end. An evaluation appeared on the tables, and people were busy packing up and soon after started drifting out. Ideally, you may aspire to a much more effective ending that brings true closure.

What should you accomplish at the end of the training session, particularly on the last day? Here are five things you should consider:

1. **Be sure that expectations were met.** If you asked participants to identify their expectations of the session and you listed them on a flipchart page, refer to that now to show that you have addressed all their needs. And if you haven't, tell participants the plan for doing it later. Ensure that you have answered all the questions that were posted in the parking lot and that you have contact information for everyone with whom you will follow up after the session. You may also wish to review the session objectives.

2. **Deliver a final group exercise.** The experience should bring closure to the session. It could be a way to wrap up loose ends, share contact information, close out a topic, bring finality to the theme, or finalize the last step in the topic. One trainer told me that she presented a real-time video at the end. She started by taping the empty room before participants arrived and then continued to tape segments of the training session. She showed the tape at the end of training. You could also take digital shots and put together a collage. In the past, I've taken 35mm pictures, delivered them to a one-hour photo shop, and distributed them at the end of the session so that participants could take them home. I've done some creative things including

   ◆ Reading a Dr. Seuss book, *Oh! The Places You Will Go!*
   ◆ Asking participants to evaluate what they still need to learn, identifying another participant who could help them and exchanging contact information with each other.
   ◆ Having participants design and deliver "Thank You Diplomas" to each other, an opportunity for participants to thank other participants for their contribution to the session.

3. **Evaluate the experience.** Sure you can do the typical smiley sheet evaluation. In fact, you probably must complete it. But there are other things you could experiment with:

- You could conduct a verbal feedback session. This could be done in one large group using a simple T-grid with "what went well?" and "what could we have done better?"

- Instead of participants rating the training, the session, and the facilities, have them rate themselves. See Tool 8.1 for a format that I've used in the past. I like to use this one at the end of day one of a multi-day session. It helps learners see that the participants have some responsibility in making the training work.

- Have participants answer open-ended questions that encourage them to implement what they learned. The questions could include some of these:

  - What was the most valuable experience you had?
  - What was the most important thing you learned?
  - What is the significance of what you experienced and what you learned?
  - How will you implement what you experienced and what you learned?

4. **Develop action plans.** Action plans can be written or verbal. A written action plan might be a list of questions that participants complete relating to the content and their next steps. Tool 8.2 offers an example of a personal planning document. You will probably want to customize it for your session. Figure 8.1 is an example of an action plan you may wish to use. You might also consider creating a continuous action plan that participants complete as they move through the session. For example, at the end of each module you might allow 10 minutes of reflection time in which participants address what they learned and how they might implement what they learned on the job. A verbal action plan is actually a spoken statement of what each person will do as a result of the training. You simply

TOOL 8.1
Participant Self-Evaluation

My Participation Self–Evaluation

Teamwork

1.	I volunteered willingly.	Yes	No
2.	I supported new ideas.	Yes	No
3.	I appreciated the diversity brought by others.	Yes	No
4.	I was enthusiastic about the opportunity to learn with my colleagues.	Yes	No
5.	I encouraged silent members to provide input.	Yes	No
6.	I worked to improve teamwork in _____.	Yes	No

Communicating and Listening

1.	I listened to the end of statements before jumping to conclusions.	Yes	No
2.	I listened for understanding.	Yes	No
3.	I helped keep the group focused.	Yes	No
4.	I asked for clarification when necessary.	Yes	No
5.	I remained 100-percent focused during discussions.	Yes	No
6.	I contributed willingly to the discussions.	Yes	No
7.	I helped the group reach compromises and understanding.	Yes	No
8.	Before speaking, I considered the value I would add.	Yes	No

Learning/Dialogue/Thinking

1.	I identified and challenged my own assumptions.	Yes	No
2.	I remained open and receptive to all concepts.	Yes	No
3.	I tried to see the issues through the other person's eyes.	Yes	No
4.	I explored alternatives besides my own opinion.	Yes	No
5.	I incorporated individuals' perspectives in my analysis.	Yes	No
6.	I tried to think from an "all department" perspective.	Yes	No
7.	I was attentive to others' preferences.	Yes	No

STEP 8

TOOL 8.2
Personal Planning Page

What are the most important things I've learned from this program?

As a result of what I've learned, what specific things do I want to implement?

What obstacles or barriers might prevent me from implementing what I want?

Who could help me overcome these barriers and how could he or she do this?

How will I know that I've been successful? What measures will I use?

By what date do I want to have implemented the above ideas and plans?

FIGURE 8.1
Action Plan Template

Objectives	Strategies	Resources	Who	Review Date

ask volunteers to share what they intend to do as a result of the workshop, making a commitment to the rest of the people in the room.

5. **Say "goodbye."** Ending the session may include other things, such as administering tests and distributing certificates. And there is one other step that for me is the sign of a professional trainer and that is to say goodbye to each participant and offer to support them in any way

End early. Your participants will thank you for it.

that you can following the training session. This is often most easily done at the door as participants leave.

You owe it to your participants to provide the best training session ever. Make it the best it can be from start to finish.

Personal Steps to Success

1. Pull openings from three training sessions that you deliver. Give them the PUNCH test. How well do your sessions address the five important aspects of a good opening?

2. Observe another trainer and watch specifically for transitions that worked and transitions that didn't work or were nonexistent. Translate what you observed to your own training improvement opportunities.

3. Select one of the books from the Activities, Games, and Surveys list in the Resources for Trainers section at the back of this book. Thumb through your selection, looking for activities that you can tailor to create a new icebreaker or closing activity for your next training session.

STEP **8**

Don't Forget Classic Techniques That Enhance Learning

OVERVIEW

- Providing ideas that save time
- Providing suggestions to increase energy and enthusiasm
- Listing tips, tricks, and techniques that increase the chances of success
- Changing direction in a training session

Applying tips, tricks, and techniques may suggest that some kind of magic or smoke and mirrors uphold training. This could not be further from the truth. Step 3 makes it quite clear that the recipe for successful training depends on your preparation and practice. But there is more.

Tricks, tips, and techniques add the spice to your training recipe. And we all know that a dish without spice can be reliable, but bland and boring. However, a recipe of just spice, without substance, is useless.

This step shares ideas that will help you save time in your training sessions, while at the same time increasing the level of energy and creating a more enthusiastic environment. This assortment of tips, tricks, and techniques will be both informative and fun for you, your training colleagues, and your participants.

This Step Is Important for Success

This step is important for success because you want your training session to be the best possible. You can purchase lots of books that will tell you how to use ISD to design a perfect training session or how to make a great presentation. But all the answers aren't in books; sometimes you just need to be creative. This step provides you with a good dose of creativity.

Everyone loves a new idea whether you are the participant on the receiving end, or the trainer on the giving end. This step helps you enhance the learning by suggesting new techniques you may not have tried. However, this step does not try to give you all the answers, but instead provides a few examples so that you can create your own tips and techniques to improve your training sessions.

This step offers a mixture of ideas that have been tried and have worked in many instances. This step alone does not lead to success, but knowing and using the information you glean from these examples will make you aware of how to create your own tips and techniques.

Every job has tips, tricks, and techniques that ensure that the work is completed in the best way possible. Training is no different. The handful of tips found on these pages have all come from watching other training experts. Trainers generally want other trainers to succeed, so we share these ideas to lead you to successful training.

Creativity and Training

Many trainers like to be creative in the design and/or the delivery of training. I especially like to try out new things—not necessarily insanely strange things, but just new and interesting enough so that they are unique and different for the participants and me. It is one way that I keep my energy up.

Listed here are a few creative ideas I've used in the past. You are free to try them out as I have written them, but what they are really intended to do is to nudge you to think about ideas that might add a creative touch to the way you currently conduct some part of your training. For example, we all use case studies to allow participants to think through an issue or identify the lessons learned. In the text that follows you will see how I altered its purpose a bit.

Case Study

I expanded the use of a case study for one training design by using it as the review activity for the first day of a two-day session. I wrote the case study providing plenty of information about a fictitious organization. The issues that the fictitious organization faced could be addressed with the knowledge that was presented in the training session on the first day. The participants became consultants and worked in small groups to make recommendations to the senior leadership of the organization. The result:

- ◆ Participants had a chance to review what they learned that day.
- ◆ The case study generated interesting dialogue among the small groups.
- ◆ Participants heard how others viewed the issues.
- ◆ Participants put into practice what they learned.
- ◆ The facilitator had an opportunity to observe how well participants picked up the day's content.

This was a twist on the normal way a case study is used. It continues to be successful, meeting all the objectives, and everyone leaves the session with a sense of closure.

Make a Point

I use this technique a lot. I design a short demonstration that makes an important point that I do not want people to forget. Many of my colleagues do this with magic tricks. I've never done magic, but you could certainly consider it. For example, I make a point when I train people about writing instructions of any kind, such as task analysis or communicating how to do anything. To do this, I pass out small index cards and place a piece of cream pie on a plate and a fork sitting atop a napkin on the front table. I then ask them to write the directions for eating the piece of pie. Timing is important, because you want to do this just before a break. As people complete their directions dismiss them for a break. During the break, read the instructions they have written and select several that will make your point. When everyone returns from break I ask someone to read the instructions I have pulled out, and I demonstrate **exactly** what they say. For example if it says, "sit down" I will sit down on the floor; if it says, "pick up the fork," I will pick it up by the tines; if it says, "pick up the napkin" first, I will purposefully pick up the napkin making the fork fall to the floor. Well, you get the idea, and it becomes quite funny when I am told to "put the pie in my mouth" without having been told to open my mouth. The results:

◆ Participants learn the importance of not making assumptions.

◆ Participants observe firsthand what happens when communication is not clear.

◆ An important point is made.

◆ Everyone has fun.

A similar exercise can be developed to make many different points. One per training session is usually enough.

Reviewing Material

I am partial to implementing what was learned as a means of reviewing the material. Therefore, I like to present a situation in which participants have hands-on practice for reviewing the content. For example, in a training design session the culmination for the participant may be to design a course. Therefore, I ask participants to bring enough information into the session so that they can work on something they will actually use. For a speaking class, participants prepare to deliver a speech that they will give in the near future. There are times, however, when the training session is filled with knowledge gained in addition to skills. In those cases, I like to create crossword puzzles to review the material. You will find great crossword software at www.crosswordweaver.com.

Techniques with a Twist

As trainers we need to use some techniques on a recurring basis. You will do your participants a favor by learning new ways to present the same tools. One tool that comes to mind is brainstorming. We all need to use brainstorming for various topics. Here are a few new twists on the old technique of brainstorming:

◆ Participants could work alone and list ideas before the group portion begins.

◆ Participants could work in pairs to develop a list as quickly as possible, and then the pairs would share the ideas in a large-group round robin.

◆ Start with a blank sheet of paper and have each person write down one idea and pass it to the left. The next person reads the idea and writes another one. Move the pages quickly. When participants cannot think of an idea, they will write "pass." Stop rotating the pages when half of the responses are "pass." Participants read ideas from the sheets they ended with, and a facilitator writes the ideas on a flipchart.

◆ Everyone begins with a stack of index cards. Each person writes one idea on one index card. At the signal all cards are passed to the right. Participants read the idea that was passed to them, take a new index card, and write another idea. At the signal all cards are again passed to the right. This continues until all the cards make one complete revolution around the group. The ideas can now easily be sorted into categories.

◆ Use two or three recorders on two or three different flipcharts to keep the ideas flowing more rapidly.

◆ Post flipcharts on the wall. Have groups of four or five brainstorm as many ideas as they can in five minutes.

STEP 9

Have the groups move to the next flipchart leaving one person behind to quickly review the list with the new participants and then have the new groups add ideas to the list.

All of these are just slightly different from generic brainstorming. However, your participants will meet each suggestion with a renewed enthusiasm for brainstorming.

You can reinvigorate almost any technique that you currently use. Go through your training designs and delivery notes with a keen eye.

Use Themes for Planning and Design

Add fun and creativity to your session by using a theme. The theme becomes a metaphor for the topic. For example, you might use a building theme, journey or trip theme, jungle theme, tool theme, sport theme, investment theme, exercise theme, or hundreds of others. Carry out the theme, with the words you use, the examples you offer, graphics on materials and visuals, how you form small groups, and sometimes even with the snacks you serve.

POINTER

Find ways in your training design and delivery to spice things up a bit with a simple twist, different supplies, or a creative direction.

For example, I used a financial theme during a team-building session. I used words such as "invest in your team," activities to identify the "deposits and withdrawals" people make in teams, found paper plates and napkins that had money pictured on it, placed miniature Payday candy bars on the table in the afternoon, used "dollar" pencils and notepads, and several other things to keep the theme alive.

How do you come up with a theme? I don't try to force them. They usually just come to me as I am designing a training session. A sentence I use, an image I've added to the PowerPoint presentation, the way an author phrases something in a book—any of these might become the inspiration for a theme. Ideas come from everywhere. You just need to be open to them when they come your way. A theme can be fun and add some interest throughout the session while tying everything together nicely.

POINTER

Keep a theme file. It might include pictures, words you've written on a napkin, cartoons, or actual objects to stimulate you the next time you are searching for a theme.

A Dozen Ideas to Form Subgroups

You often need to form small subgroups for activities, to ensure balanced participation, to encourage competition, to allow participants to learn from each other, and to increase activity and participation. Counting off is often used, but you can make it much more fun. Here are a few tricks to make even this part of training fun.

Stickers

Before the session begins, place stickers on the backs of handouts, binders, or folders for each participant. Use animals, letters, plants—whatever stickers you can find. It's even better if they match the session's theme. For example, if you want five groups, use an equal number of five different animals; if you want three groups, use an equal number of three different trees; and so on. Divide the stickers appropriately so that people will be in different teams each time and place them

POINTER

Walk through a dollar store and select 10 items that you could turn into a theme for your next few training programs. Keep them for creative inspiration.

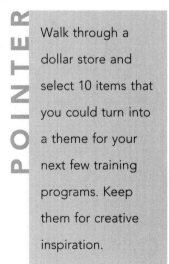

STEP 9

POINTER

Arrange participants in small groups before you provide the assignment. If you begin with the directions and then divide them into groups, many will have forgotten what they were supposed to do by the time they have found their group.

on the back of the participant materials. When it is time for a subgroup you can announce that, "all the zebras will sit here, all the rhinos can sit there . . . " and so on.

Table Tents

The sticker idea can also be used by placing them inside—or outside—table tents. Another way to use table tents is to place a different-colored marker at each person's spot and repeat the colors at each table. Form teams by the color of marker participants' used to write their names on the table tent. You can collect all the table tents and then redistribute them on the tables and have participants move to the table where their table tent was placed.

Puzzling

Create puzzles that incorporate a message about the topic. Cut them into pieces. Hand out the pieces and ask participants to form groups based on the puzzle pieces they have. You could purchase small puzzles. Party stores sometimes have blank puzzles (used for invitations) you could use.

Count Off Creatively

Count off but do it in an unusual way, in a foreign language, or backwards, or by twos.

Vocal Variation

If you don't care how many groups you have or how many people are in each, have everyone in the group think of something that is likely to involve 10 or fewer items. For example, their favorite colors, the last digit in their telephone numbers, their favorite flavor of soda, the sound of the first vowel in their names, and so on. Have everyone stand and say the word he or she has selected until others have said the same word, and form a team out of those with like responses.

Odds and Ends

You can distribute almost anything to enable participants to form subgroups. Consider wrapped candy, small toys, small tools, crayons, shaped erasers, participant material such as colored pencils or folders, party favors, cards, different sport bubble gum cards, and so on.

Personal Information

Divide participants into small groups based on something pertaining to them, for example, the month or season of their birthday or birth order in the family (oldest, youngest, middle, only child).

Pairing Up

Sometimes you want to form pairs. You could ask participants to find someone who has the same color of shoes, the same first letter of their first or last name (or for added fun their middle names), or same color of hair. You could make it different, too, such as someone who has a *different* color of eyes from yours or shoes with or without laces.

Line Up

If the information is consecutive such as birthdays, alphabetical order of names, or height, have participants line up in order and then split the line at the point of a new subgroup.

STEP **9**

Sing a Song

Write familiar song titles on index cards, such as "Mary Had a Little Lamb," "Happy Birthday," and others, until you have as many as the number of groups you want and pass them out. Everyone stands and begins to sing the song they have drawn until they find the rest of their singing teammates. You can also use several well-known advertising slogans such as "You're in good hands" or "Melts in your mouth, not in your hands" or "Plop, plop, fizz, fizz"; use sounds made by body parts such as clapping, snapping, stomping; or use business phrases such as "you've got mail."

Categories

Write the names of characters or items that belong together, one name per sticky note. For example, characters could be Dorothy, the Tin Man, Toto, Scarecrow, and the Wizard. Another category could be trees, and the names would be oak, maple, walnut, pine, and ash. Place one sticky note on the back of each participant and have group members locate the others who belong in their categories.

Where in the World?

Use location to divide the group into subgroups. For example, you could ask everyone to head toward the corner of the room that would be the direction they would take to go home, "as the crow flies." You could present several vacation locations such as seaside, lake, mountains, or city, and have them select a vacation spot. You could ask them where they would like to go for a foreign vacation such as England, Australia, or the Far East. You might ask what part of the country they were born in, for example, Midwest, South, or West Coast. Remember that you need to be prepared for wide variation in the number of members in each subgroup. You will need to be prepared if having an approximate number of people in each of these groups is important. You can always combine two small groups or singles. You can also split a larger group in half.

One of the advantages of using personal information or preferences is that even though it is not related to the topic, participants will learn something about the others in the group, which
leads to more trust, improved communication, and greater sharing
of ideas during the session. Forming subgroups doesn't need to
mean "counting off." It can actually be an energizer in itself. Make
a pact with yourself to never count off again!

When to Change Direction

Every so often a participant will ask a question that is not directly
related to the content you are delivering. However, you realize
that it is important to the participant who asked the question and
in some cases you look around and see other heads nodding as
well. In some instances the question may even be a prerequisite to
understanding the current content in the session.

When is it appropriate to stray from the content in the training session? How do you respond to individual participant needs
and not get off track? Is it ever permissible to change the agenda?
How do you manage to deliver all the training content as well as
answer the questions and concerns from participants?

It's all about balance. As a trainer you need to consider several
things: time, relevance, and how to make the decision.

Time

The considerations include how tight is your training schedule? Are
you ahead or behind schedule? Has time been built into the agenda
to accommodate additional information? How much time is needed
to address the issue? Is there a quick answer?

STEP 9

Consider first if there is some way that you can respond immediately but quickly. This means providing a short answer or recom-
mending a book, article, reference, or a referral to another expert.

You could ask the participant to place the question in the parking lot for later discussion if it will take more than a minute to respond and would break into the current content flow.

In the end, if a particular training session generates many questions and most of the questions are related to the topic and participants genuinely need answers, you might consider building in time to respond. This could be done in a couple of ways. First, you might want to just create more flexibility in the schedule when you design or redesign the session to answer questions as they arise. A second method that I've used successfully is to build in a Problem-Solving Clinic near the end of the session. Compile all the questions throughout the session, add others that participants generate, prioritize them as a group, and assign the top priorities to small groups to answer.

Relevance

Is the question relevant to the content? Should the information be added to the training in the future? Is the question politically charged? Does the question relate to the participants' ability to transition the content to the workplace?

If the question does not seem to be of interest to many participants, offer to answer the question during the break, at lunch, or after the session. If it is likely to be a longer discussion than can be covered during a break, you may also offer to call or meet with the participant the next day or next week.

If the concern or question is politically charged, you may not want to answer it at all. You can always use the agenda as your ally in this case, saying something like, "That's an interesting topic. Our agenda is too tight to even scratch the surface."

However, if the question relates directly to the participants' ability or inability to transition the content to the workplace, you have a situation that may be worthy of changing the agenda. Read more about this in the next section.

Decision-Making Process

Who should make the decision, the trainer or the participants? What role does the agreement you have with the client play in the decision? What other ways exist to meet the participants' needs? How can you make an appropriate decision?

You may have other ways to address new critical issues that do not mean making changes to the content. For example, you could meet with the interested participants after class (either the same or another day). You could send materials to the participants. You could offer to hold a follow-up session. You could offer to prepare materials and coordinate a conference call.

On rare occasions (although it does occur), a critical topic may arise that you feel needs to be addressed. Even though the topic is not on the agenda, you and most of the participants feel that it is important for the ultimate success of the training session so participants will be able to implement the results. If it will take a great deal of time, is related to the content, and is of interest to at least most of the participants, you may choose to add the new content. This is a serious decision, and you have several choices:

- ◆ You could shorten some of the material and substitute the new content.
- ◆ You could change some of the material, perhaps deleting an activity.
- ◆ You could delete some of the material and substitute the new content.

I don't generally recommend the third choice unless you have 100 percent buy-in from all of the participants—no matter how important the new material. This is the one instance in which I would involve the participants in the decision. Your client (boss or customer) has contracted with you to deliver specific content. Think about this one.

In the end it is really your decision. You'll need to weigh the consequences. Most important, don't forget to consider a redesign

STEP **9**

TABLE 9.1
Meeting Planning Assessment

When you find yourself in a sticky situation in which the participants' needs do not match the content, you have options about how to handle additional information:

◆ Respond immediately if time permits and the response is short.

◆ Place the issue in the parking lot.

◆ Offer to answer at another time if the issue is of interest to only a few.

◆ Offer to follow up at a later date for one person or a group.

◆ Follow up with a conference call.

◆ Offer additional support in the form of books, articles, or other people.

◆ Shorten some of the material and substitute the new content.

◆ Change some of the material, perhaps deleting an activity, having smaller groups address more than one topic at a time.

◆ Delete some of the material and substitute the new content (with 100-percent agreement from the session participants).

◆ Add a problem-solving clinic near the end of the training design to address multiple questions at the same time.

◆ If content was overlooked, consider changing the design.

POINTER

Keep a copy of Table 9.1 in your facilitator's guide so it is ready for the next time participants' needs diverge from the agenda.

if indeed critical content has been overlooked. Table 9.1 summarizes your options. Remember, you are responsible for balancing participants' needs with the content.

Finally, whether you stray for a couple of minutes or an hour, be sure that you have a plan to transition back into the content.

Providing Support After the Training Session

How can you provide support after the training session has ended? Step 2 presents several thoughts on how you can help to ensure that the training meets a business goal. Some of the ideas in Step 2 are follow-up actions. It might be wise to review these follow-up items at this time. Once you are certain that this training is the answer to meeting a business goal, you can do some additional things to ensure that the participants have all the tools they need to transfer the training to the workplace. These traditional ideas will be good reminders and jumping off points for ideas of your own:

- job aids, such as correctly filled in forms
- photos of a correct process or final product
- reference books
- schematic drawings
- electronic performance support systems (EPSS)
- mentoring
- coaching
- reminder calls or emails
- flow charts or task lists
- personal action plan or phased action plans
- participant buddies
- follow up with additional tools
- follow-up exams or questionnaires
- return report to trainer or supervisor about implementation
- training others about what was learned.

You do not have to be the one who creates the follow-up job aid. As an activity in your next session have participants create a job aid. This is a good way for them to review the content and put it to practical use.

This step has presented a hodgepodge of suggestions to provide you with ideas that save time and increase energy, enthusiasm, and determine the results of any

POINTER

Follow-up is the single most important step you can take to encourage participants to implement what they have learned.

STEP 9

training session. You may find some of these tips, tricks, and techniques a bit of a stretch, but they are sure to increase the chances of success for your training sessions. I hope they have inspired you to try something a bit more spicy during your next training session.

Turn up the heat; add some spice to your next training session. The fusion of the ideas in this step with your well-designed training session will be a recipe for success.

Personal Steps to Success

1. Select a portion of one of your training sessions that contains important information yet seems to drag. Determine why it isn't as vibrant as the rest of the training session. Then identify a couple of tricks or techniques that you could use to liven it up.

2. Develop a job aid and create a follow-up plan for its implementation in your next training session. How can you help ensure that the knowledge and skills transfer to the workplace?

3. Implement at least one new technique every day that you conduct a training session. You will expand your knowledge, impress your participants, and increase your enthusiasm overall.

Get Involved—Helping Others Learn Is Fun and Rewarding

Finally! You have reached the most exciting step to success—your professional development. Have you ever thought about all the skills in which you need to be proficient? I sometimes get exhausted just thinking about everything I need to do to ensure a successful training session. From needs assessment to evaluation, this is no cookie-cutter job. Every day is different. Every design is different, every delivery is different, and every participant group is different. We are so lucky to have these differences because they challenge us to grow and develop.

This is what makes the job of trainer so exciting, but it is also what necessitates trainers to be lifelong learners.

This step explores what it means to become a lifelong learner and offers a list of ways that you can do this. It also will give you some ideas for creating your professional development plan. But the process doesn't end there. It's impossible to say that you

STEP 10

should become a lifelong learner without maintaining your enthusiasm and giving back to the profession.

Thomas Jefferson said, "If we did all the things we are capable of, we would literally astound ourselves." Sadly, most of us will never know all that we are capable of. Becoming a lifelong learner is a step in the right direction. Go ahead. Take Jefferson's challenge. Astound yourself!

This Step Is Important for Success

At first blush, the reasons this step is important may be more obscure than those for the first nine steps. I can think of at least two reasons. You may think of others.

First, developing your skills and knowledge allows you to maintain your place on the cutting edge. By doing so you are providing the kind of training your employer and your participants expect and deserve.

Second, and most important, you owe it to yourself to continue to develop your skills and increase your knowledge. Staying in touch with the changes and the excitement of the profession will keep you enthusiastic and passionate about what you do. We should all enjoy what we do and have pride in ourselves and in our profession.

I have never believed that anyone should have to get up and go to work in the morning. We should all love our jobs so much that we get up and go to play every day. This step is important because it keeps us vibrant and knowledgeable about the work we do.

Becoming a lifelong learner, creating a professional development plan, maintaining the spark of inspiration, and giving back to the profession are actions that all professionals owe to their employers, clients, colleagues, those new to the profession, and especially themselves. This is a personal and professional step to ensure successful training.

Becoming a Lifelong Learner

Patricia Cross's 1981 book, *Adults as Learners,* described three features that embody the lifelong-learning process, including

- a more holistic concept of growth or education than that which has been used in traditional formal education
- a wider view of providers and settings for education than merely schools (what she terms the learning society)
- the active agency or self-directedness of the learner throughout the life span.

Today's learner embraces all of what Cross suggests. We as trainers need to lead the effort, especially the aspect of self-direction.

To be a true model of success and professionalism, trainers, and more broadly workplace learning and performance (WLP) professionals, need to model the importance of lifelong learning. We need to learn continually. Learning is paramount to achieve all that you are capable of.

I once read that most people achieve only a third of their potential. Successful professionals in any position achieve much more than a third of their potential because they continue to learn and grow. What do lifelong learners do?

- They assess where they are compared with where they want to be and determine a plan to get there.
- They improve their processes continuously. They identify new ways to work that are better and more efficient and implement them.
- They are on the cutting edge of their industry trends. They are aware of state-of-the-art practices as well as the fads of the day; know about the training gurus and

STEP 10

their philosophies; and have knowledge of the professional organizations, journals, and newsletters that help them stay abreast of developments in the field.

◆ They are in the know about their customers (internal and external). They keep up to date about all the things that are happening to their customers.

To incorporate this list into your professional life means a lifetime of learning for anyone in the field of training and development. You have an obligation to your employer and your customers to improve your knowledge and skills continually. The rapid changes in the world can turn today's expert into tomorrow's dolt if the person fails to keep up. How can you do it?

Take Stock and Take Action

Step back and take stock of where you are and where you want to be. Determine some measure of success, drive a stake in the ground, and head for it. You can establish measures that include both knowledge and skills. Next, identify a developmental plan for continued growth. Consider several strategies.

Attend Learning Events

At a minimum, attend your professional organization's annual conference. It may be expensive, but you owe it to your clients to invest in yourself. I can think of no more enjoyable way to learn than to go to a great location, meet new people, renew past acquaintances, and attend sessions in which presenters discuss new ideas and approaches. You may very likely go home with a fistful of business cards belonging to others whom you can tap into to continue your learning.

To get the most out of your attendance, be sure to network. Don't sit on the sidelines or retreat to your room during breaks. You will not gain all the value that you can. Instead, go where the action is. Be the first to say hello. Introduce yourself to others and be interested in who is there. Identify common interests and experiences. Trade business cards. If the person has asked you for something or if you want to follow up after the conference, jot a note on the back of the business card as a reminder.

POINTER

Make a list of all the things you would like to learn—professionally and personally. If you work internally, ask your supervisor for suggestions. If you work externally, list things you can learn that would benefit your clients.

Attend Virtual Learning Events

My email inbox is filled with offers to "attend" webinars, teleconferences, and webcasts. Many are free, the rest have a small price tag. All will stimulate learning, produce knowledge, and encourage thinking.

Go Back to School

You may not need an MBA, but courses at the graduate level are critical. Take courses in finance, marketing, human performance technology, or organizational change. Take a class to get yourself up to speed in technology.

Ask Others

Ask for feedback from others on a regular basis. Ask for it from friends, colleagues, and participants. Ask your internal customers about their most pressing concerns. Although this is not related to you specifically, the learning may be fascinating, and this will enhance your relationship.

Join an Association

One of the best ways to stay current in the field is to be an active member of your professional association. I often hear trainers say they "can't afford the dues." They have it all wrong. They can't afford *not* to join! Your ability to keep up with the profession depends on staying in touch. Affiliation with a national professional association or group is critical to maintaining your professional awareness. Through the group, you will be kept informed of learning events. This membership is an investment in *you*. If you won't invest in you, who will?

POINTER

The next time you attend a conference or a local chapter association meeting take a number of business cards (you set the goal) and exchange all of them with others. Follow up after the meeting with those from whom you can learn. Offer to take them to breakfast or lunch.

Get Involved

Do more than just write a check for your annual association dues. In addition to attending the organization's annual conference, volunteer for a committee. You will be involved in the work of the profession, communicating with other professionals and working with colleagues. It's an enjoyable way to continue to learn!

Network

Sometimes a professional organization will provide a networking list that is designed to provide you with contacts in your geographic location. If not, form your own network. Networking is one of the best ways to continue to learn or, at the very least, to learn what you ought to learn!

Study on Your Own

Reading is one of my favorite methods of learning. Get on the mailing lists for ASTD Press and Jossey-Bass/Pfeiffer to stay up to date on the most recent training and development publications. Subscribe to and read your professional journals. Read general business magazines such as *Fortune, Business Week,* or the *Harvard Business Review.* Read the same publications your customers read to keep yourself informed about the industry. Read new, cutting-edge journals such as *Fast Company.* While working on another project, I learned that WLP professionals are voracious readers. Dana Robinson, for example, reads half a dozen journals each month, and Jack Phillips subscribes to almost 40 publications.

Discover Resources

Visit your local technology training organization. Check out the classes they offer and other available resources they can lend you. Visit your local bookstore. Browse the shelves looking for trends in the industries you serve and business in general. Thumb through all new books about training to determine if they should be on your bookshelf. Sign up for an online service. The World Wide Web is a dynamic source of professional development resources. Sites provide information as well as link you to other related sites. Sign up for newsletters and webzines in your particular field. The *New York Times* and your other favorite newspapers will deliver the headlines to your computer each day if you subscribe.

Co-Train with Others

Training with a colleague is a unique way to learn from someone else in the profession. It allows you to observe someone else, elicit feedback, and learn from the experience of working together. Invite colleagues to observe you during a facilitating, consulting, or training situation. Ask them to observe specific things. Sit down afterward and listen to everything your colleagues say. Ask for suggestions for improvement.

STEP **10**

Create Mentoring Opportunities

Meet with other professionals to discuss trends in the profession. Identify someone in the training field whom you would like as a mentor. Then ask the person if that would be possible. My mentor and I meet for breakfast four to six times each year. I pay for our meals. This has become the best $20 investment I've ever made. I'm investing in myself. Identify where the experts hang out. Then go there. Sometimes you'll find a mentor through a related association or an informal group. Other seasoned professionals and those with different experience can offer you priceless advice.

Aspire to Being the Best You Can Be

Your session participants and customers expect you to be on the leading edge of advances in the field. You have an obligation to them and to yourself to learn and grow. Learning is an ongoing process, even if you are at the top of your profession. Often it is what you learn *after* you know it all that counts. This section offers suggestions on ways to maximize your potential.

Professional Delivery Standards

Establish standards for yourself that are high enough to keep you on your training toes and that encourage continual reaching. Guarantee that your training will be the highest quality your participants have ever experienced. Put quality ahead of everything else—you won't go wrong. Set your standards high and never compromise them. Quality: First, last, and everything in between.

Establish Your Training Values

Are you cognizant of what you believe about training? If a reporter from the *New York Times* pushed a microphone in front of you and

An Example of a Trainer's Value Statement

As a trainer I

◆ remember that training is all about the learner

◆ respect my learners

◆ set the learner up for success

◆ ensure that learners know why the content is important and how it can benefit them

◆ believe that the participants' knowledge is much greater than mine

◆ recognize that unlearning may need to occur prior to learning

◆ believe that my success is dependent on my learners' successes.

asked you what your philosophy was with regard to training, could you easily express exactly what you believe?

You may want to take time to create your own training values statement. Call it what you like—a philosophy, a belief statement, your guiding principles—that doesn't matter. As a trainer, spend time identifying what you believe about training to create your own training values statement. The example in the pointer may get you started.

Consider Certification

Certification or accreditation is available in many fields as a way of learning and achieving a professional standing in the profession in which you train. The accreditation could be related to your profession, such as a Certified Public Accountant (CPA) or a Certified Electrical Engineer (CEE). It could also relate to your specific training area, such as a Certified Professional in Learning and Performance (CPLP), Certified Speaking Professional (CSP), International Coach

STEP **10**

Federation (ICF) Credential, Certified Professional Facilitator (CPF), or a Certified Management Consultant (CMC).

Check these websites for certification information. Go to www.nsaspeaker.org for a CSP; www.coachfederation.org for an ICF credential, www.imcusa.org for a CMC; www.iaf-world.org for a CPF; or www.cplp.astd.org for a CPLP.

Improve Your Communication Skills

Although last, communication is certainly not least. The skill that goes awry the most often in any situation is communication. Your ability to listen, observe, identify, summarize, and report objective information is key to your success as a productive trainer. Equally important are your abilities to persuade, offer empathy, solve problems, and coach others. These other communication skills are requirements for a successful trainer. Constantly work at improving your communication skills.

If you like being a trainer, don't stop there. Be a master trainer. Be a respected, knowledgeable trainer. Be a *successful* trainer. Be a *highly professional* trainer. Be all the things that you are capable of being. *Astound* yourself!

Creating Your Professional Development Plan

We've discussed why becoming a lifelong learner is important and have considered techniques that will enable you to continue to learn. Who better than a trainer to create a professional development plan? If you are like most trainers, you probably help other individuals regularly think through and create their individual development plans (IDPs). Your organization most likely expects you to create your own professional development plan.

You can refer back to your last plan if you wish, but I'd like to challenge you to stretch a bit. Becoming a lifelong learner requires you to move beyond what you will learn as a trainer. Create a plan that is holistic. You may use the categories listed in Table 10.1. These are the categories I use, with the addition of one more, business.

POINTER

An IDP will help you stay focused.

Maintaining the Spark

What do you want to be when you grow up? Since we've mentioned lifelong learning, it's time to decide if you are in the right profession. Are you inspired by what you do? Are you enthusiastic about what you do? Are you self-motivated by what you do? Life is too short to spend it doing something you don't like.

What did you dream about as a child? What did you want to do? Do you still have that dream? Are you doing it now?

If training is your dream and you find that you don't have the energy or enthusiasm you once had, perhaps you have taught the same training session one too many times. Perhaps the travel schedule or the long hours are getting you down. What can you do to make every training session seem as exciting as your first? Here are a few ideas:

- ◆ Experiment with activities you've never tried before, perhaps a relay race or Thiagi's funneling. Grab a book written by Thiagi or Mel Silberman for some great ideas.
- ◆ If you have never conducted a true experiential learning activity, incorporate one into your next session. Pfeiffer

STEP 10

TABLE 10.1
Holistic Development Plan

Use this example as a model. You may wish to add or delete categories. The ultimate goal, however, is to incorporate all aspects of your life. Establish a timeline that you feel comfortable with: a one-, three-, five-, or 10-year plan. The key is to make your plan work for you.

Category	Goal	Resources	Date
Professional			
Personal			
Financial			

STEP
10

Health				Hobbies				Family				Pleasure				

and Jossey-Bass (and especially the Pfeiffer Annuals) are excellent resources for you to use.

◆ Do something that is just a little different. Show a movie and serve popcorn. Put bubble gum on the tables and have a bubble-blowing contest as an energizer. Ask participants to complete an activity using a crayon. Hold a discussion outside.

◆ Invite a guest speaker to conduct a section of the training session.

◆ Co-facilitate your next session. Plan for new learning methods two trainers could conduct that one cannot, for example, set up a debate, try a point–counterpoint discussion, or use role play.

◆ Review the evaluations from a previous training session and select something based on the comments that could be improved. Then identify and incorporate an improvement.

◆ Conduct research about the topic so that you can incorporate new data and information.

◆ The day before the session, pull out your smile file (the one filled with all the glowing remarks about you, thank you cards, awards, and pictures) and read through it to remind yourself of how much others appreciate what you do.

◆ Take a digital camera to the session. Take pictures of some of the activities and the participants. Be sure to get at least one picture of everyone. Create a slide show and share it at the end of the training session.

◆ Select a reward—get a massage, purchase a new perfume, stop for a beer with the guys—and treat yourself after the session.

Maintain Your Personal Spark

Yes, it is important to maintain your professional spark. It is equally important to maintain your personal spark. Do you maintain the spark with physical activity by gardening, exercising, walking, dancing, playing sports, practicing Pilates, or yoga?

- with relaxation through meditation, getting a massage, getting enough sleep, listening to music?
- through awareness of your eating habits, drinking enough water, eating nutritious food?
- with awareness of your emotions by being positive, expressing yourself, keeping a journal, having fun, celebrating?

POINTER

Make a list of everything that inspires and rejuvenates you. Put it where you will see it every day.

- through replenishing your mind by daydreaming, reading, learning something new, observing beauty?

Each of these has a rejuvenating effect that will make you a better person as well as a better trainer.

Find the passion in your life. As trainers we need to have our own spark because we light fires for so many others. Love what you do and do what you love.

Giving Back to the Profession

Throughout your career you have most likely received support from others. Now it is time to give back to the profession. Here's a list to get you started:

- Volunteer your services to a government, civic, or non-profit organization.
- Volunteer to serve on a committee for your professional association.
- Speak at a local professional chapter meeting.
- Mentor someone new to training.
- Volunteer your services to a civic group.
- Volunteer to speak to your local high school or community college.
- Send a thank you card to someone who has contributed to the profession.
- Start a scholarship fund.

STEP 10

Giving back to the profession is good for the soul. Find a way to volunteer today.

Becoming a lifelong learner is exciting. It is sure to put passion back in your life! Remember, this is an investment in you. If you won't invest in you, who will? I hope we all have an attitude similar to Michelangelo's:

Ancora imparo.
(Still I am learning.)

—*Maxim of Michelangelo*
(1475–1564)

Personal Steps to Success

1. What do you need to know to be a skilled and competent trainer? I suggest that you examine ASTD's Competency Model to remind yourself of the breadth and depth of the profession of the workplace learning and performance professional.

2. Create your personal training values statement to better focus your thoughts and beliefs about what you do.

3. Create a holistic developmental plan as suggested in this step (see Table 10.1). Share it with someone and state your timeline and objectives. Ask if you and your colleague can meet on a regular basis to review your progress.

4. Subscribe to a new journal for a year—one that your customers read. Schedule appointments with your customers to discuss some of the articles and the implications they may have for how you can better support the customer.

5. Think back to your childhood dream. What did you want to be? Have you achieved your goal? It's never too late.

STEP 10

CONCLUSION:

Continuing Your Journey

As you read the *10 Steps to Successful Training,* I hope that you understand why I chose these particular steps as the ones that lead to successful training. Perhaps as you worked your way through the book you have initiated changes in your training methods to implement or improve some areas described within the steps. I would love to hear about what you are doing. In addition, if you have thoughts about different steps that need to be included in the "top 10," I'd love to hear about those as well.

I also hope that I have inspired you in some small way to do three things:

◆ Take professional action based on information in one or more of the steps. Whether they are the only steps that should be included or not, I don't think you can disagree the information they provide is extremely important. But reading about steps to improve your training will not take you very far. Each of the steps requires action on your part. You may wish to share them with your training colleagues to make appropriate changes in how you design or deliver. Or you may wish to redesign some of the programs you currently offer to clients. Whatever you choose, I do hope that at least a couple of these steps have spurred you to act. What improvements have you made in your products and services?

- Identify personal actions you are taking to make a difference in your life as a trainer. Training is perhaps one of the best jobs in the world. We get to contribute directly to our organizations' success, develop and influence others to be more productive and successful at their jobs and in life in general, and continue to learn and try new things as a part of our profession. And, in addition, we get paid to do it! Given that we have an important role to play, we each owe it to ourselves and our participants to continue to improve our skills. What actions are you taking to improve yourself?

- Make a commitment to continue to learn more about the training field and your chosen professional niche. So much new happens every day, especially with brain research into how we learn; information as to why some people are more successful at a task than others; how brain exercises can help performance; the relationship among learning, memory, and plasticity; and so on. We will all be amazed at what science will uncover over the next years. With all that is happening in this area alone, how can you not want to engage in continuing to learn about the field? What commitments have you made to future plans for life-long learning?

With that in mind, I want to draw your attention to the Resources for Trainers found on the next few pages. Because this book isn't long enough to include everything you need for successful training and because many people much smarter than I am have written fabulous books about the subject, you will find an extensive list of resources in the back of this book.

You'll find several classics on the list mixed in with those that are fresh off the press. I've provided my favorite suggestions if you are looking for content to supplement each of the 10 steps. I am sure other great books will join these on bookshelves everywhere.

However, for now here's what I recommend for each of the 10 steps.

Step 1: Malcolm Knowles's *Self-Directed Learning* from 1975 is a fast read and will help you see how far we've come in the industry. Read any of Robert Mager's books to also help you understand training's roots.

Step 2: Two books stand out for this step, Dana and Jim Robinson's *Moving from Training to Performance* and *The Six Disciplines of Breakthrough Learning* by Cal Wick and his co-authors.

Step 3: What you need to remember as you are reading this is that the focus of this step is really adult learning theory—not design and development. Read Knowles's *The Adult Learner: A Neglected Species* and consider it also a must read to understand training's roots.

Step 4: No one book stands out here. You'll find ideas in books by Jean Barbazette, Saul Carliner, Karen Lawson, and George Piskurich.

Step 5: Try *Training from the Heart* by Barry Lyerly and Cyndi Maxey for this step.

Step 6: Grab one or two of Thiagi's books listed here. He is certainly the expert in the area of facilitation. You should not miss Mel Silberman's *Handbook of Experiential Learning*.

Step 7: Jean Barbazette provides you with all the necessaries in *The Art of Great Training Delivery*.

Step 8: Bob Pike is the outstanding author in this area. Check his website for his latest book or even better, subscribe to his newsletter. If you haven't paged through *90 World-Class Activities by 90 World-Class Trainers,* you owe it to yourself to do so, every big name in training has contributed his or her all-time favorite activity to the book.

Step 9: Read one of Sharon Bowman's books for a boatload of tips and tricks. She models what she writes about, so catch her at ASTD's next International Conference and Exposition.

Step 10: There is no book specific to this topic, though lots of goal-setting, self-help books exist. If you want to read a book to enhance your knowledge, I suggest either the *ASTD Handbook for Workplace Learning Professionals* or *Presenting Learning* by Tony Bingham and Tony Jeary.

I hope you will pick up several of these books. Even if you've read them in the past, books often take on a new meaning the second time you read them, after you have additional experience. I also hope this book has provided you with an informative, easy-to-follow path to the 10 steps to successful training.

Resources for Trainers

So many things to learn as a trainer! So little time! This resource list provides you with a list of books, websites, suppliers, and organizations to help you reach success. Enjoy!

Professional Organizations

American Society for Training & Development (ASTD)
1640 King Street
Box 1443
Alexandria, VA 22313
(800) 628-2783, www.astd.org

Association for Quality (ASQ)
P.O. Box 2055
Milwaukee, WI 53201-2055
(800) 733-3310 fax (414) 765-7219, www.asq.org

The Canadian Society for Training and Development Organization
110 Richmond Street East, Suite 206
Toronto, Ontario M5C 1P1, Canada
(416) 367-5900, www.cstd.ca

Instructional Systems Associations (ISA)
The Association of Learning Providers
12427 Hedges Run Drive #120
Lake Ridge, VA 22192
(703) 730-2838, fax (703) 730-2857, www.isaconnection.org

International Alliance for Learning (IAL)
2380 Buford Dr., Suite # 106-374
Lawrenceville, GA 30043-7638
(800) 426-2989, (678) 518-4034, fax (770) 277-3649, www.ialearn.org

International Federation of Training & Development Organisations, Ltd. (IFTDO)
7 Westbourne Road
Southport PR8-2HZ, England
(44) (704) 67994, www.iftdo.org

International Society for Performance Improvement (ISPI)
1400 Spring Street, Ste 260,
Silver Spring, MD 20910
(301) 587-8570 fax (301) 587-8573, www.ispi.org

The National Speaker's Association (NSA)
1500 S. Priest Drive
Tempe, AZ 85281
(480) 968-2552, www.nsaspeaker.org

Organizational Development Network (ODN)
76 S. Orange Avenue, Suite 101
South Orange, NJ 07079-1923
(201) 763-7337, www.odnet.org

Society for Human Resource Management (SHRM)
1800 Duke Street
Alexandria, VA 22314-3499
(703) 548-3440, (800) 238-7476, www.shrm.org

Toastmasters International
P.O. Box 9052,
Mission Viejo, CA 92690
(949) 858-8255, www.toastmasters.org

United States Distance Learning Association

P.O. Box 5129

San Ramon, CA 94583 (925) 606-5160, www.usdla.org

Books

Training—General Topics

Barbazette, J. (2006). *The Art of Great Training Delivery*. San Francisco, CA: Jossey-Bass/Pfeiffer.

Barbazette, J. (2004). *Instant Case Studies: How to Design, Adapt, and Use Case Studies in Training*. San Francisco, CA: Jossey-Bass/Pfeiffer.

Barbazette, J. (2001). *The Trainer's Support Handbook*. New York: McGraw-Hill.

Bellman, G. (1990). *The Consultant's Calling: Bringing Who You Are to What You Do*. San Francisco, CA: Jossey-Bass.

Bernthal, P., K. Colteryahn, P. Davis, J. Naughton, W. Rothwell, and R. Wellins. (2004). *ASTD 2004 Competency Study: Mapping the Future*. Alexandria, VA: ASTD Press.

Bersin, J. (2008). *The Training Measurement Book: Best Practices, Proven Methodologies, and Practical Approaches*. San Francisco, CA: Pfeiffer.

Bersin, J. (2004). *The Blended Learning Book*. San Francisco, CA: Jossey-Bass/Pfeiffer.

Biech, E., ed. (2008). *ASTD Handbook for Workplace Learning Professionals*. Alexandria, VA: ASTD Press.

Biech, E. (2007). *The Pfeiffer Book of Successful Team-Building Tools* (2nd ed.). San Francisco, CA: Jossey-Bass/Pfeiffer.

Biech, E. (2005). *Training for Dummies*. Hoboken, NJ: Wiley.

Bingham, T., and T. Jeary. (2007). *Presenting Learning: Ensure CEOs Get the Value of Learning*. Alexandria, VA: ASTD Press.

Bossidy, L., and R. Charan. (2002). *Execution: The Discipline of Getting Things Done*. New York: Crown Business Books.

Bowman, S. (2005). *The Ten-Minute Trainer: 150 Ways to Teach It Quick and Make It Stick!* San Francisco, CA: Pfeiffer.

Bowman, S. (2003). *Preventing Death by Lecture*. Glenbrook, NV: Bowperson Publishing.

Bowman, S. (2002). *Presenting with Pizzazz*. Glenbrook, NV: Bowperson Publishing.

Bozarth, J. (2008). *From Analysis to Evaluation: Tools, Tips, and Techniques for Trainers*. San Francisco, CA: Pfeiffer.

Brinkerhoff, R. (1999). *Achieving Results from Training*. San Francisco, CA: Jossey-Bass.

Broad, M., and J. Newstrom. (1992). *Transfer of Training*. Reading, MA: Addison-Wesley.

Carliner, S. (2003). *Training Design Basics*. Alexandria, VA: ASTD Press.

Cross, P. (1981). *Adults as Learners*. San Francisco, CA: Jossey-Bass/Pfeiffer.

El-Shamy, S. (2004). *How to Design and Deliver Training for the New and Emerging Generations*. San Francisco, CA: Jossey-Bass/Pfeiffer.

Eitington, J. (2002). *The Winning Trainer* (4th ed.). Woburn, MA: Butterworth-Heinemann.

Hale, J. (2002). *Performance-Based Evaluation: Tools and Techniques to Measure the Impact of Training*. San Francisco, CA: Jossey-Bass/Pfeiffer.

Justice, T., and D. Jamieson. (1999). *The Facilitator's Fieldbook*. New York: AMACOM.

Kirkpatrick, D.L. (2006). *Evaluating Training Programs: The Four Levels* (3rd ed.). San Francisco, CA: Berrett-Koehler.

Knowles, M. (1994). *The Adult Learner: A Neglected Species*. Houston, TX: Gulf Pub. Co.

Knowles, M. (1975). *Self-Directed Learning*. Chicago: Association Press.

Knowles, M., E. Holton, R. Swanson, and E. Holton (2005). *The Adult Learner: The Definitive Classic in Adult Education and Human Resource Development* (6th ed.). Boston, MA: Amsterdam Press.

Kolb, D. (1991). *Learning Styles Inventory*. Boston, MA: McBer & Company.

Lawson, K. (2006). *The Trainer's Handbook* (2nd ed.). San Francisco, CA: Jossey-Bass/Pfeiffer.

Lawson, K. (1998). *Train-the-Trainer: Facilitator's Guide*. San Francisco, CA: Jossey-Bass/Pfeiffer.

Lucas, R. (2003). *The Creative Training Idea Book*. New York: AMACOM.

Lyery, B., and C. Maxey. (2000). *Training from the Heart*. Alexandria, VA: ASTD Press.

Mager, R. (1999). *What Every Manager Should Know About Training* (2nd ed.). Atlanta, GA: Center for Effective Performance.

McCain, D., and D. Tobey. (2007). *Facilitation Skills for Training*. Alexandria, VA: ASTD Press.

McCarthy, B., and J. O'Neill-Blackwell. (2007). *Hold On, You Lost Me!: Use Learning Styles to Create Training That Sticks*. Alexandria, VA: ASTD Press.

Meier, D. (2002). *The Accelerated Learning Handbook: A Creative Guide to Designing and Delivering Faster, More Effective Training Programs*. New York: McGraw Hill.

Millbower, L. (2003). *Showbiz Training*. New York: AMACOM.

Phillips, J. (1997). *Return on Investment in Training and Performance Improvement Programs*. Alexandria, VA: ASTD Press.

Phillips, J. (1997). *Handbook of Training and Evaluation and Measurement Methods*. Alexandria, VA: ASTD Press.

Phillips, J., and P. Phillips. (2005). *ROI at Work*. Alexandria, VA: ASTD Press.

Pike, R. (2003). *Creative Training Techniques Handbook* (3rd ed.). Amherst, MA: HRD Press.

Pike, R. (2000). *One-on-One Training: How to Effectively Train One Person at a Time*. San Francisco, CA: Jossey-Bass/Pfeiffer & Creative Training Techniques Press.

Piskurich, G. (2003). *Trainer Basics*. Alexandria, VA: ASTD Press.

Piskurich, G. (2000). *Rapid Instructional Design*. San Francisco: John Wiley.

Piskurich, G. (1999). *The ASTD Handbook of Training and Delivery* (2nd ed.). New York: McGraw-Hill.

Robinson, D., and J. Robinson (2008). *Performance Consulting: A Practical Guide for HR and Learning Professionals* (2nd ed.). San Francisco: Berrett-Koehler.

Robinson, D., and J. Robinson (1998). *Moving from Training to Performance*. San Francisco, CA : Berrett-Koehler.

Rosania, R. (2003). *Presentation Basics*. Alexandria, VA: ASTD Press.

Rossett, A. (1997). *First Things Fast: A Handbook for Performance Analysis*. San Francisco, CA: Jossey-Bass/Pfeiffer.

Rothwell, W., and H.C. Kazanas (2004). *Mastering the Instructional Design Process* (3rd ed.). San Francisco, CA: Jossey-Bass/Pfeiffer.

Rothwell, W., and H.C. Kazanas. (2004). *Improving On-The-Job Training: How to Establish and Operate a Comprehensive OJT Program* (2nd ed.). San Francisco, CA: Jossey-Bass/Pfeiffer.

Russell, L. (2005). *Training Triage: Performance-Based Solutions Amid Chaos, Confusion, and Change.* Alexandria, VA: ASTD Press.

Silberman, M. (2007). *The Handbook of Experiential Learning.* San Francisco, CA: Pfeiffer.

Silberman, M. (2006). *The 2006 ASTD Training and Performance Sourcebook.* Alexandria, VA: ASTD Press.

Silberman, M. (1998). *Active Training* (2nd ed.). San Francisco, CA: Jossey-Bass/Pfeiffer.

Stolovitch, H., and E. Keeps (2002). *Telling Ain't Training.* Alexandria VA: ASTD Press.

Tamblyn, D. (2003). *Laugh and Learn.* New York : AMACOM.

Thiagarajan, S. (2003). *Design Your Own Games and Activities.* San Francisco, CA: Jossey-Bass/Pfeiffer.

Ukens, L. (2001). *What Smart Trainers Know: The Secrets of Success from the World's Foremost Experts.* San Francisco, CA: Jossey-Bass/Pfeiffer.

Wick C., R. Pollock, A. Jefferson, and R. Flanagan (2006). *The Six Disciplines of Breakthrough Learning: How to Turn Training and Development into Business Results.* San Francisco, CA: Pfeiffer.

Zemke, R., and Kramlinger, T. (1982). *Figuring Things Out.* Reading, MA: Addison-Wesley.

Activities, Games, and Surveys

Barca, M., and Cobb, K. (1993). *Beginnings & Endings.* Amherst, MA: HRD Press.

Biech, E. (2008). *Trainer's Warehouse Book of Games: Fun and Energizing Ways to Enhance Learning.* San Francisco, CA: Pfeiffer.

Biech, E. (2006). *90 World-Class Activities by 90 World- Class Trainers.* San Francisco, CA: Pfeiffer.

Burn, B. (2000). *Assessments A to Z: A Collection of 50 Questionnaires, Instruments, and Inventories.* San Francisco, CA: Jossey-Bass/Pfeiffer.

Carosilli, M. (1998). *Great Session Openers, Closers, and Energizers.* New York: McGraw-Hill.

Editors. (1972–present). *The Annual* series. San Francisco, CA: Jossey-Bass/Pfeiffer.

Gordon, J. (2004). *Pfeiffer's Classic Inventories, Questionnaires, and Surveys for Training and Development.* San Francisco, CA: Jossey-Bass/Pfeiffer.

Kapp, K. (2007). *Gadgets, Games, and Gizmos for Learning: Tools and Techniques for Transferring Know-How from Boomers to Gamers.* San Francisco, CA: Pfeiffer.

McLaughlin, M., and S. Peyser. (2004). *The New Encyclopedia of Icebreakers.* San Francisco, CA: Jossey-Bass/Pfeiffer.

Pike, B., and L. Solem. (2000). *50 Creative Training Openers and Energizers.* San Francisco, CA: Jossey-Bass/Pfeiffer.

Scannell, E.E., and J. Newstrom, (1998). *The Big Book of Presentation Games.* New York: McGraw-Hill.

Scannell, E.E., and J. Newstrom. (1983-1998). *Games Trainers Play Series.* New York: McGraw-Hill.

Silberman, M. (2004). *The Best of Active Training: 25 One-Day Workshops.* San Francisco, CA: Jossey-Bass/Pfeiffer.

Sugar, S., and J. Whitcomb (2006). *Training Games: Simple and Effective Techniques to Engage and Motivate Learners.* Alexandria, VA: ASTD Press.

Tamblyn, D., and S. Weiss (2000). *The Big Book of Humorous Training Games.* New York: McGraw-Hill.

Thiagarajan, S. (2007). *Card Games by Thiagi: A User's Guide.* San Francisco, CA: ASTD Press.

Thiagarajan, S. (2006). *Thiagi's 100 Favorite Games.* San Francisco, CA: Pfeiffer.

Thiagarajan, S. (2005). *Thiagi's Interactive Lectures: Power Up Your Training With Interactive Games and Exercises.* Alexandria, VA: ASTD Press.

Ukens, L. (2004). *The New Encyclopedia of Group Activities.* San Francisco, CA: Jossey-Bass/Pfeiffer.

Ukens, L. (2000). *Energize Your Audience: 75 Quick Activities That Get Them Started and Keep Them Going.* San Francisco, CA: Jossey-Bass/Pfeiffer.

VanGundy, A. (1998). *101 Great Games & Activities.* San Francisco, CA: Jossey-Bass/Pfeiffer.

West, E. (1997). *201 Icebreakers.* New York: McGraw-Hill.

Creativity and the Brain

Biech, E. (1996). *The ASTD Trainer's Sourcebook, Creativity & Innovation.* New York: McGraw-Hill.

Cameron, J.(1992). *The Artist's Way: A Spiritual Path to Higher Creativity.* New York: G.P. Putnam's Sons.

Herrmann, N. (1995). *The Creative Brain*. Lake Lure, NC: The Ned Herrmann Group.

Lucas, R.W. (2007). *Creative Learning: Activities and Games that REALLY Engage People*. San Francisco, CA: Pfeiffer.

Lucas, R.W. (2003). *The Creative Training Idea Book: Inspired Tips and Techniques for Engaging and Effective Learning*. New York: AMACOM.

Millbower, L. (2000). *Training with a Beat: the Teaching Power of Music*. Sterling, VA: Stylus.

Von Oech, R. (1998). *A Whack on the Side of the Head* (3rd ed). New York: Warner.

e-Learning

Arch, D., and S. Ensz. (2000). *Web-Based Interactive Learning Activities*. Amherst, MA: Recommended Resources.

Aldrich, C. (2004). *Simulations and the Future of Learning: An Innovative (and Perhaps Revolutionary) Approach to e-Learning*. San Francisco, CA: Jossey-Bass/Pfeiffer.

Allen, M. (2008). *e-Learning Annual*. San Francisco, CA: Pfeiffer.

Allen, M. (2006). *Creating Successful e-Learning: A Rapid System For Getting It Right the First Time, Every Time*. San Francisco, CA: Pfeiffer.

Carliner, S. (2002). *Designing E-Learning*. Alexandria, VA: ASTD Press.

Clark, R. (2003). *E-Learning and the Science of Instruction: Proven Guidelines for Consumers and Designers of Multimedia Learning*. San Francisco, CA: Jossey-Bass/Pfeiffer.

Clark, R.C. (2007). *Developing Technical Training: A Structured Approach for Developing Classroom and Computer-based Instructional Materials*. San Francisco, CA: Pfeiffer.

Driscoll, M. (2002). *Web-Based Training: Creating e-Learning Experiences* (2nd ed.). San Francisco, CA: Jossey-Bass/Pfeiffer.

Hofmann, J. (2004). *Live and Online!* (with CD-ROM). San Francisco, CA: Jossey-Bass/Pfeiffer.

Islam, K. (2008). *Podcasting 101 for Training and Development: Challenges, Opportunities, and Solutions*. San Francisco, CA: Pfeiffer.

Lee, W., and D. Owens. (2004). *Multimedia-Based Instructional Design*. San Francisco, CA: Jossey-Bass/Pfeiffer.

Piskurich, G. (2004). *Getting the Most from Online Learning*. San Francisco, CA: Jossey-Bass/Pfeiffer.

Piskurich, G. (2003). *Preparing Learners for e-Learning*. San Francisco, CA: Jossey-Bass/Pfeiffer.

Shank, P., and A. Sitze. (2004). *Making Sense of Online Learning: A Guide for the Beginners and the Truly Skeptical*. San Francisco, CA: Jossey-Bass/Pfeiffer.

Graphics and Design

Arch, D., and I. Torgrimson. (1999). *Flip Chart Magic*. Amherst, MA: HRD Press.

Brandt, R. (1997). *Flip Charts*. San Francisco, CA: Jossey-Bass/Pfeiffer.

Lucas, R.W. (1999). *The Big Book of Flip Charts*. New York: McGraw-Hill.

Millbower, L. (2002). *Cartoons for Trainers*. Sterling, VA: Stylus.

Sonneman, M. (1997). *Beyond Words: A Guide to Drawing Ideas*. Berkeley, CA: Ten Speed Press.

Monthly Publications

ASTD Infoline, American Society for Training & Development, 1640 King Street, P.O. Box 1443, Alexandria, VA 22313, www.astd.org

T+D, American Society for Training & Development, 1640 King Street, P.O. Box 1443, Alexandria, VA 22313, www.astd.org

Training Magazine, Nielsen Business Media, 770 Broadway, New York, NY 10003, www.trainingmag.com

Products

Assessment Instruments, Simulations, and Games

HRD Press
22 Amherst Road
Amherst, MA 01002
(800) 822-2801 www.hrdpress.com

Human Synergistics
39819 Plymouth Road
Plymouth, MI 48170
(313) 459-1030 www.humansynergistics.com

Pfeiffer/Jossey-Bass
989 Market Street
San Francisco, CA 94103
(800) 274-4434 www.pfeiffer.com

HRDQ
2002 Renaissance Blvd. #100
King of Prussia, PA 19406
(610) 292-2614 www.hrdq.com

Clip Art

Click Art, PrintMaster, Print Shop
Broderbund
88 Rowland Way, Novato, CA 94945
(415) 895-2000 www.broderbund.com

Jupiterimages
5232 E. Pima St.
Suite 200C
Tucson, AZ 85712
1-800-482-4567 www.clipart.com

COSMI

2600 Homestead Place

Rancho Dominguez, CA 90220

(310) 886-3510 www.cosmi.com

Key Click Art

The Learning Company

1 Athenaeum Street

Cambridge, MA 02142

(800) 845-8692 www.learningco.com

Creative Training Products

Bob Pike Group

7620 West 78th Street

Minneapolis, MN 55439-2518

(800) 383-9210 www.bobpikegroup.com

Creative Presentation Resources, Inc.

P.O. Box 180487

Casselberry, FL 32718-0487

(407) 695-5535 (800) 308-0399 www.presentationresources.net

Trainer's Warehouse

89 Washington Avenue

Natick, MA 01760

(508) 653-3770 (800) 299-3770

www.trainerswarehouse.com

Graphic Art Materials

Chartpak

(800) 788-5572 www.chartpak.com

Staedtler, Inc.

P.O. Box 2196

Chatsworth, CA 91311

(800) 776-5544 www.staedtler-USA.com

Music

Classical Archives, LLC
200 Sheridan Ave, Suite 403
Palo Alto, CA 94306
www.classicalarchives.com

Network Music, LLC
15150 Avenue of Science
San Diego, CA 92128
www.networkmusic.com

Offbeat Training®
(407) 256-0501 www.offbeattraining.com

The Music Bakery
7522 Campbell Road, #133-2
Dallas, TX 75248
www.musicbakery.com

Paper Supplies

Baudville
5380 52nd Street, S.E.
Grand Rapids, MI 49512-9765
(800) 728-0888 www.baudville.com

Idea Art
P.O. Box 291505
Nashville, TN 37229-1505
(800) 435-2278 www.ideaart.com

Paper Direct
P.O. Box 2970
Colorado Springs, CO 80901-2970
(800) 272-7377 www.paperdirect.com

Presentation Equipment and Accessories

Clearanswer Limited
11604 Carlsbad Road
Reno, NV 89506
(775) 845-7626 www.clearanswer.com

Graphic Products

P.O. Box 4030

Beaverton, OR 97076-4030

(800) 788-5572 www.graphicproducts.com

Neuland North America Ltd.

P.O. Box 6745

Great Falls, MT 59406-6745

(888) 713-2333 www.neuland.biz

Props, Toys, and Training Tools

Creative Learning Tools

P.O. Box 37

Wausau, WI 54402

(715) 842-2467 www.creativelearningtools.com

M&N International

P.O. Box 64784

St. Paul, MN 55164-0784

(800) 479-2043 www.mninternational.com

Oriental Trading Company

P.O. Box 2659

Omaha, NE 68103-2659

(800) 526-9300 www.orientaltrading.com

Videos and Films

American Media Inc.

4900 University Ave.

West Des Moines, IA 50266-6769

(800) 262-2557

CRM Films

2215 Faraday Avenue

Carlsbad, CA 92008-7295

(800) 421-0833 www.crmlearning.com

Licensing

American Society of Composers, Authors, and Publishers (ASCAP)
(Music)
One Lincoln Plaza,
New York, NY 10023
(800) 952-7227 www.ascap.com

Broadcasting Music, Inc. (BMI)
(Music)
10 Music Square East
Nashville, TN 32703
(800) 925-8451 www.bmi.com

Copyright Clearance Center, Inc.
(Photos, electronics, books, newsletters, magazines, newspapers)
222 Rosewood Drive
Danvers, MA 01923
(978) 750-8400 www.copyright.com

Seminars

Center for Accelerated Learning
David Meier, Director
1103 Wisconsin Street
Lake Geneva, WI 53147
(262) 248-7070 www.alcenter.com

Creative Training Techniques International, Inc.
Robert W. Pike, CSP, President
7620 West 78th Street
Edina, MN 55439
(800) 383-9210 www.cttbobpike.com

Instructional Development Workshop
Darryl L. Sink & Associates, Inc.
60 Garden Court, Suite 101
Monterey, CA 93940
(800) 650-7465 www.dsink.com

Partners in Change, Inc.
2547 Washington Road, Suite 720
Pittsburgh, PA 15241-2557
(412) 854-5750 www.partners-in-change.com

INDEX

ABOUT THE AUTHOR

Elaine Biech is president and managing principal of ebb associates inc, an organization development firm that helps organizations work through large-scale change. She has been in the training and consulting field for 30 years and works with business, government, and nonprofit organizations.

Biech specializes in helping people work in teams to maximize their effectiveness. Customizing all of her work for individual clients, she conducts strategic planning sessions and implements corporate-wide systems, such as quality improvement, reengineering of business processes, and mentoring programs. She facilitates topics such as coaching today's employee, fostering creativity, customer service, time management, stress management, speaking skills, training competence, conducting productive meetings, managing change, handling the difficult employee, organizational communication, conflict resolution, and effective listening.

She has developed media presentations and training materials and has presented at dozens of national and international conferences. Known as the trainer's trainer, she custom designs training programs for managers, leaders, trainers, and consultants. Biech has been featured in dozens of publications, including *The Wall Street Journal, Harvard Management Update, The Washington Post,* and *Fortune* magazine.

As a management and executive consultant, trainer, and designer she has provided services to FAA, Land O'Lakes, McDonald's, Lands' End, General Casualty Insurance, Chrysler, Johnson Wax, PricewaterhouseCoopers, American Family Insurance, Marathon Oil, Hershey Chocolate, Federal Reserve Bank, U.S. Navy, NASA, Newport News Shipbuilding, Kohler Company, ASTD, American Red Cross, Association of Independent Certified Public Accountants, the University of Wisconsin, the College of William and Mary, ODU, and hundreds of other public- and private-sector organizations to prepare them for the challenges of the new millennium.

Biech is the author and editor of more than four dozen books and articles, including *ASTD Handbook for Workplace Learning Professionals*, 2008; *The Consultant's Quick Start Guide*, 2nd ed., 2008; *The Business of Consulting*, 2nd ed, 2007; *Thriving Through Change: A Leader's Practical Guide to Change Mastery*, 2007; *Successful Team-Building Tools* 2nd ed, 2007; *90 World-Class Activities by 90 World-Class Trainers*, 2007 (named a Training Review Best Training Product of 2007); nine volume set of ASTD's *Certification Study Guides*, 2006; "12 Habits of Successful Trainers," ASTD *Infoline*, 2005; *The ASTD Infoline Dictionary of Basic Trainer Terms*, 2005; *Training for Dummies*, 2005; *Marketing Your Consulting Services*, 2003; *The Consultant's Legal Guide*, 2000; *Interpersonal Skills: Understanding Your Impact on Others*, 1996; *Building High Performance*, 1998; *The Pfeiffer Annual for Consultants* and *The Pfeiffer Annual for Trainers (1998 - 2008); The ASTD Sourcebook: Creativity and Innovation— Widen Your Spectrum;* 1996, *The HR Handbook,* 1996; *Ten Mistakes CEOs Make About Training,* 1995; *TQM for Training,* 1994; "Diagnostic Tools for Total Quality," *Infoline,* 1991; *Managing Teamwork,* 1994; *Process Improvement: Achieving Quality Together,* 1994; *Business Communications,* 1992; *Delegating for Results,* 1992; *Increased Productivity Through Effective Meetings,* 1987; *Stress Management, Building Healthy Families,* 1984. Her books have been translated into Chinese, German, and Dutch.

Biech received her B.S. from the University of Wisconsin-Superior in business and education consulting, and her MS in human resource development. She is active in ASTD at the national level, is a lifetime member who has served on the 1990 National Conference Design Committee, was a member of the National ASTD Board of Directors, and was the Society's Secretary from 1991-1994. Biech initiated and chaired Consultant's Day for seven years and was the International Conference Design Chair in 2000. In addition to her work with ASTD, she has served on the Independent Consultants Association's (ICA) Advisory Committee and on the Instructional Systems Association (ISA) board of directors.

Biech is the recipient of the 1992 National ASTD Torch Award, the 2004 ASTD Volunteer-Staff Partnership Award, and the 2006 ASTD Gordon M. Bliss Memorial Award. She was selected for the 1995 Wisconsin Women Entrepreneur's Mentor Award. In 2001 she received ISA's highest award, The ISA Spirit Award. For the past 12 years she has been the consulting editor for the prestigious publication, *Training and Consulting Annuals,* published by Jossey-Bass/Pfeiffer.